The Sa...
Within

The Definitive Guide to Eliminating Self Sabotage

BY

MATT HUDSON

About the Author

Born in Newcastle upon Tyne, North East England in 1967, Matt is an eternal optimist. From birth he had severe hearing problems (conductive deafness), which was undiagnosed until he was an adult. He actually sees himself as fortunate to have this dis **"ability"**, as it has heightened his other senses to such a degree that he has developed a unique and uncanny gift. Matt is able to 'see' when you have lost rapport with yourself, by picking up the incongruent messages that are the cause of your dis-ease.

Matt is an exceptionally intuitive spirit who has the capacity to facilitate and support change. A powerful conduit, he supports you to reconnect with your true self. His unique and eclectic approach incorporates fun, compassion and spontaneity. He is on a continual quest for self-development, looking to affirm every individual's right, to be seen as an equal and to fulfil their true potential.

"Whatever the problem, a part of you already knows the answer; my job is to have you connect with that part and provoke you into growth and change!"

❧

Thank You

To my many influencers

Richard Bach, for writing Jonathan Livingstone Seagull, this was my first awakening to how it all fits together. Lieutenant Columbo, who I modelled for years to hone my own brand and style of coaching. Wilf Proudfoot, for introducing me to the work of Virginia Satir, the other detective that I aspire to be. Franz Anton Mesmer, for being the first real hypnotist and Milton H Erickson, for a lifetime, devoted to making hypnosis a modern day reality. Wayne Dyer, Deepak Chopra, Caroline Myss, Marian Williamson and Louise Hay, for keeping my soul and spirit connected. Richard Bandler, John Grinder, Robert Dilts, Steve Andreas and Tad James as well as many others within the world of NLP. Mr Ted Hayes, my old P.E teacher, whose passion has always inspired me. Glenn Skevington and his wife Hilary Chapman for supporting me on my many workshops. My associates Henk and Carla Beljaars, Eva Hyllstam, Kath Temple and Paul Dearlove for challenging me to become more. Rusty Fischer my writing coach, now I know what a table of contents is for J. To Tom Brennan and Karen Kirkbride for the final edits and Norma Foster for an unparalleled attention to detail in the final proof. To my many friends whom I haven't mentioned by name, as it will take ages. Shelle Rose Charvet, for your time and energy you are a gem. John Overdurf, for being the trainer that I am aspiring to be.

♋

Forever Thankful

To my darling wife Sonya, for being my partner on the rollercoaster. My wonderful sons Alan, Karl and Kurtis for tempering my metal. My mother Edith Lavinia and my father Charles Nelson Hudson together they let me run unbridled and allowed me to dream. My brothers John George (Geordie), you gave me hope and Charles Nelson for teaching me about diversity and equality. My sister Margaret and brother in law Bob, you two have always been there for me. Anthony Hall, Sonya's brother, for the front cover, "Tony, you rock!" My many clients, who have consistently inspired me to learn more about the condition called life, from which we all suffer, at some point or another.

∽

And to you,
The reader for daring to challenge your status quo,
Carpe diem.

∽

Forward

It is my pleasure to introduce you to Matt Hudson's unique take on how you can transform limitations into assets. When I met Matt years ago, the first thing I noticed was the twinkle in his eyes. He was curious, smart, and fun to be around. Whilst obviously competent, he did so without taking himself too seriously. I like that Spirit a lot. It's refreshing. You'll find this same refreshing Spirit in this book. As you turn the pages, it may rub off on you too. (That is not a *suggestion* by the way, just an observation.)

This book pulls no punches. It is written with honesty, humility, wit and competence. Most of all, it is written in a way that draws from the experience of this man's inner journey to be all he is, and his outer journey to help others to do the same.

Why *Read this Book*?

"Life is what happens while you're busy making other plans." John Lennon said that. What he didn't say is that we often don't even follow through on the plans we were busy making!

The following is pretty familiar territory for most of us humans:

Ever resolved to lose that extra weight and haven't? Then, how about getting the gym membership for a year, but the first two weeks seems to turn out to be the year?

Ever realize you aren't doing what you love, but you're doing a whole lot of what you don't love. How about deciding to "not overreact" or get stressed-out? You might even have learned to keep it in so you appear to be calm, but on the inside you know you're not.

Ever feel afraid to just "go for it, for something you are passionate about, but worried about failing?

How about worrying too much about what others think? Come on, we've all had stuff like this happen at one time or another.

Sometimes it is really obvious, and sometimes it is really subtle. Sometimes we can avoid it. Sometimes we can't stand another minute of it.

How do we get ourselves into these kinds of patterns, and more importantly how do we get ourselves out of them? The answers might surprise you. You might think this book is about self-sabotage and you'd be right.... in knowing... that it is really NOT. It is about how to transform a "saboteur" into an "ally."

In this book, Matt gives you the straight scoop on how and why sometimes we can "successfully" snag failure from the jaws of success, and more importantly, what we can do to turn failure inside-out to create success. It is about getting to know the bigger part of who you are at any moment of your life: your unconscious mind.

A Primer on the Evolution of the Brain, the Unconscious Mind

If your conscious mind is your current awareness, then your unconscious is everything else you're not aware of within you. "It" regulates your "bodily" functioning from immune, to digestive, to respiration, blood pressure; you name it - along with all of your emotional and mental functions, which happen automatically. "Automatically" is the operative word here. The brain, the organ between our ears, loves to learn (make associations) and make those learnings automatic as fast as possible.

At the deepest level the brain is built for survival and most of these programs run unconsciously. We tend to store and remember threats more vividly and intensely than "the good things" in life. This is well documented in neuro-science. It is the so-called "Negativity Bias". But why? Wouldn't the world be a better place if we took in the good as well as the not so good? Well maybe now, but tens of thousands of years ago that was not the case. And the news is we still have that same hardwiring in our brains!

Just imagine: You are in the Serengeti. Each day you must be vigilant. Survival is job one. You have to pay attention to potential threats. (Remember your brain wants to learn things as fast as it can and make those learnings automatic.) So in this environment you need to avoid threats like being eaten by a lion, but you are also looking for opportunities, food, water, and attractive mates to reproduce your band.

If you fail to recognize and respond quickly to a threat, one mistake is all it takes - lights out! If you can't find opportunities that day because you are busy successfully avoiding threats, you may miss a meal and sex, but all is not lost. You will at least live another day to seek those opportunities.

We still have this hard wiring. Perhaps our boss uses some nasty tonality, but our unconscious responds more like when a lion is attacking us. What had been our "survival" part now has become our "saboteur" part. It was an adaptation that worked before. But now it no longer fits the context. There's more to the story, but for now feel good in knowing there are ways to retrain your brain in this book.

What Stops Us from Being All We Can Be?

For roughly the first 7 years or so our lives, our brain, and every other organ is collecting information to determine how we need to adapt to be living in the environment we are in. We are closely watching, listening, feeling, smelling, and tasting everything we can from our surroundings. We are sensory-based beings at this point. We have not developed higher thinking functions like reasoning, analysis, and abstraction. Those higher functions don't begin to develop until about age 7 and they take a few years to become more functional. So during these early years we have an excellent ability to take things in, but have not yet developed how to buffer or filter out some of the nasty stuff that can happen in life.

Here's an example about a client I worked with, who came to me for *hypnotherapy* many years ago, who may *remind you* of someone you know. To preserve confidentiality, I'll just refer to him by his initials: *B.U.*

One day *B.U. is playing* amongst his toys that are all around him on the living room floor. There's *B.U. laughing, B.U. exploring, learning and* playing, surrounded by all sorts of things that fascinate him and he is engaged. To *B.U., this is complete freedom, fun, and creative expression.* B.U. is a happy child doing what a child that age tends to do.

Meanwhile Dad is driving home from work. He's had an awful day. Before going to work, he opens some mail he didn't have time to open the day before. It's a late payment notice from the bank. He gets to work and his boss informs him that he will have to take on more work since the company had eliminated one of his support positions. The day is a blur. With hardly time to eat, he downs double burger, extra cheese, and chips while in a meeting and later his digestive system is protesting. Traffic is a mess. By the time he gets home, he is irritable and on edge. Spent. It won't take much to set him off. He opens the front door and sees "the mess" in the living room. He bellows, "Clean up this mess! Now...What's wrong with you...You should know better..."

All of a sudden, completely unexpectedly, *B.U. the 'free child" becomes* "scared child." There are no filters to "make sense" of what is happening. *B.U., taking it all in,* doesn't yet *have the presence of mind to think,* " Oh the old man must have had a bad day at work and has a nasty case of indigestion. You know he should learn to be more assertive and also watch what he eats." No way! Instead the message is imprinted, stamped into his neurology: Dad's voice, tone, words, and look on his face, and now feeling free is glued together with fear. In his brain these neural networks are being wired together.

No logic here. Just simple time and place. Literally these two very different emotional states become wired together. This is one of the most basic proven principles in neuro-science: Neurons that fire together, wire together. As I mentioned before, we know the brain wants to make things automatic as soon as possible.

So days later when Dad comes home, the last thing B.U. wants to do is see that look on Dad's face and hear that voice tone. He learns to be on-guard and vigilant when Dad comes home from work. This becomes automatic and starts to generalize to other situations that are similar. As time goes on, he feels scared when he does things he really likes doing, but doesn't really know why. It's that "waiting for the other shoe to drop" feeling.

Now B.U. is all grown up, but he has one big issue: he can't really be himself. Every time he thinks about doing something where he's free to express himself--he gets scared something bad is going to happen. Now that he is an adult, he can come up with "good adult reasons" for why this is the case, but actually he has no idea how or why it happens. Nor does he realize how much it is holding him back.

His unconscious is just doing what it learned to do. This response is automatic and wired in. His unconscious now functions as the saboteur within. This reaction is not what B.U. wants, but it happens persistently and predictably. Once again, it was an adaptation that worked before, but now it no longer fits the context. *To B.U., it's time for a change. The good news is the unconscious mind knows how to learn quickly and make the learnings automatic. The new ways of being can become as permanent as the limitations once were. You just have to know how to do it.*

What Can You do to B.U, To Be All of Who You Are?

Well, this is where reading the book comes in!

To B.U. the next step is updating those old programs and transforming them into new productive ones. Time to roll-up the sleeves and get down to it:

Transform the Saboteur into an Ally. Let Matt be the provocateur that helps you along the way.

By John Overdurf

Certified Master Trainer of NLP

Co-developer of Humanistic Neuro-Linguistic Psychology and Hypnosis

Once upon a time between George Bailey pleading, "Take me back Clarence.... I want to live again", Dorothy Gale singing, "Somewhere Over The Rainbow" and James Tiberius Kirk asking me, "to boldly go where no man has gone before", I was learning to figure out why people would sabotage themselves.

All three had one thing that they shared and would bind them to a common purpose. They would all eventually re-alise that there was no place like home, no matter how many light years you travel. I hope that I can help you to reach your home, where you can be safe from the storm.

I've been described by many people as many different things, some good and some bad; it's the indifferent peo-ple who scare the bejesus out of me!

You now have the chance to form your own opinion and that is all I can ask of you. Behind these words there lies a heart, a spirit, and a soul, who wishes to make a connection to you. Read on and remember....

"Life is but a dream"

꿈

Contents

Life is but a dream

Introduction

*"Thought defines who you are today and can sabotage
who you could be tomorrow"*

Matt Hudson

Fair warning: This isn't just another self-help book. This is an alarm clock! It's a wake up call to ignite you and drive you into fully engaging in a wonderful life!

As the title of this book suggests, the chapters within these covers are about the Saboteur Within you and me, otherwise known as "your unconscious mind." The outcome, after reading, is that you will have a practical guidebook, which enables you to go beyond the limits your mind has created for you.

There are millions of people on this planet, many of whom will shuffle off at the expiration of their life, never having truly awoken and lived their life with purpose. "There'll be plenty of time to sleep at the other end," my Dad used to say. That was back when a much younger me was intent on lying in my bed for another hour while the whole universe was there for the taking, just on the other side of my bedroom door!

My experience working with clients over many, many years has been a constant reminder of the profound wisdom of my dad's words. It is through their stories (naturally, all names and identifying information has been changed) and my own insights and awakenings along the way that I hope to bring you into consciousness.

I had been sleeping far too long and now; watch out world, because I am wide-awake! Little did I know the incredible journey that awaited me. I wonder what adventures you will encounter on the other side of your own bedroom door. Aren't you excited to find out?

So, toward that end, I offer you my perspective on the purposeful life:

∽

The Power of Your Unconscious Mind

"To the mind that is still, the whole universe surrenders"

Lao Tzu

As you wander through this book with me, I'd like you to be aware that some of the client stories might touch a nerve or two for you and this is where you can focus your energy to help you to awaken and change. If you have had this book bought for you, then, after reading it, ask the person who gave you it which client stories remind them of you? You maybe surprised at what you learn here.

At the end of most chapters there is an exercise or two for you to participate in. If you are considering changing your life and evolving, then you had better get used to the idea of working with a friend or coach. The reason behind this will be apparent to you as you read on through the book. Basically, in order for you to make a shift, you first have to overcome your Saboteur and to achieve that, you will need someone who is on the outside of both you and the problem to give you feedback as you carry out the exercises.

Do write out the exercises. You will be surprised when you look back after a month or two to see what you had written. I have composed various explanations to help you to experience the world as I do. Although I have given you my answers, only you have control over your understanding.

☙

"For those who understand, no explanation is necessary; for those who don't understand, no explanation is possible"
(Adapted from) *Thomas Aquinas*

And before we go any further, I have not only changed the names of my clients, I've also changed their job roles, their relationships, and where necessary, I've changed their disease, sex, and age, all to avoid any of you recognising them. So, please forgive me on the book signing tour if you ask about Colin or Barbara and I stare at you blankly. Give me their story and then I can switch their names back inside the privacy of my own mind.

From cover to cover, this book holds many metaphors for change within it, and your unconscious mind will know which will have the most beneficial effects upon you. I will liken your mind to a best friend. I'm sure that you have, or have had, a friend you would normally share secrets with, telling them things that are very important to you? But what happens when you have a fall out and you are not friends anymore? You can be left vulnerable because that ex-friend is in possession of your innermost secrets and therefore has power over you that they might use against you.

Well, your unconscious mind knows all of your deepest secrets, it even keeps them from you, and it does this in order to keep you safe. I know it sounds ridiculous to think that there is a part of you that knows more about you than you do, but that's the plain and simple truth of the matter. Your very own Saboteur, who will use your fears against you in order that you remain safe and un-changed, guards your innermost secrets ferociously.

Let me assure you straight off that you have all of the answers, or rather your unconscious mind does. No matter what your presenting issue is, the answers are within you. My task is to remind you of the answers, reminding you that you have just forgotten for a while and you can look forward to a time, in your future, when you can look back to now, having realised that you have remembered who you truly are.

You see the problem isn't that you don't want to change. The problem is that often, when you try to change, you sabotage yourself and that means reading this book and doing the exercises a couple of times over, so that you can understand the highest intentions that your Saboteur looks to uphold for you.

Oh! Just in case I forget to mention it, every now and again I will use hypnotic language here and there to speak directly to your spirit, so if you find yourself puzzled every now and then, well done, that's right, you are doing it beautifully....

As we move forwards together through the book, you will notice that some of the client stories can be very emotive for you, whilst others are nice to know, but really have no reason for you to buy into them right now. And yet tomorrow, or who knows when, that extra insight might be just what you need to draw strength from. The book is structured to give you specific details about how your unconscious mind works and how it can effortlessly sabotage your health, wealth, relationships, and your life, full stop. There are a few exercises for you to use and I would suggest that you do so, with a friend, to capture external feedback about yourself. Yes, sure you can do this on your own and get good results, but what if the very thing you want to change about you is obvious to your friends and you can't see it? With that in mind I'd like to tell you about a good friend of mine who runs a gym. He is always amazed at the clients who come in and sign-up for a three-year membership. Why? Because after three weeks about 75% of them stop coming altogether. And after about three months, he's down to about **4% of those original members**. He calls it "sleeping" money because he doesn't have to do anything about it after the initial two- to three-week flurry is over except sleep and watch the money come in. You might be wondering about his moral obligations, but after thirty years in the health and fitness industry, he knows that no matter what he does; personal training, one to one, telephoning you to encourage you to come along, he's tried them all! He knows the age old saying is true, "You can lead a horse to water but you can't make him drink". So, here he is today having to accept money for a service that he knows he won't be able to deliver because his new clients will sabotage themselves. "Every now and again someone just gets it! And they transform their life." He says, "If I could bottle what they have, I could change the world!" Well reader, here is your bottle, drink deeply.

Just consider for a moment why in the world anyone would join a gym and immediately sign up for a three-year membership? It's human nature, of course. We're so excited about losing weight, about shaping up, about changing our lives, that if one year is good, then two years is better; and if two years is better, then three years is best! The only problem is; our motivation to change rarely lasts three weeks, let alone three years.

When's the most popular time to sell a three-year gym membership? January, of course! After all, it's the time for New Year's resolutions, for doing what we know is best for our mind, body, and soul.

It's also the time when our **conscious mind** is strongest. After all, we're fresh from a solid week of holiday eating; we're lazy from the winter weather, and soft from taking it too easy for too long. What's more, we consciously know that if we don't make some kind of healthy change in the beginning of the year, we're likely not to make it anytime this year.

So, it's off to the gym we go, fighting the first of the year crowds and burning our bodies sore until we drop from exhaustion back home on the couch. We can keep it up for another few days perhaps, burning a hole in our new tracksuits and wearing down our spiffy new training shoes and then... and then... reality hits.

That old voice starts creeping into our heads again, telling us:

- **"This'll never work!"**
- **"You're not cut out for this!"**
- **"You don't belong here!"**
- **"You're too old!"**
- **"Let's go back home and have some tea!"**
- **"I'm too busy at work/with the kids"**

You know that voice, don't you? It's the sound you've been hearing all your life. Often you want to change, to grow, to learn, to reach, and to stretch. And what happens? You get all excited about that new gym membership, that new class, that new boyfriend or girlfriend, that new job, and your conscious mind takes over, for a day or two at least.

Then the voice creeps in, sabotaging all your plans, making you feel weak, insecure, ineffective, and out of place. You fight it for as long as you can, struggling against your nature to succeed until, eventually, it wins out, as it always must – the little voice "wins" and that is that. No more gym, no more track suit, no more trainers.

Until next January, that is; and the cycle starts all over again.

Well, I'm here to tell you that that tiny little voice has a name: **your unconscious mind (your very own Saboteur)**. And if that tiny little voice sounds anxious, envious, unhappy, or any other emotion, that's because... it *is* your emotions!

Your unconscious wants your life to remain on whatever course you are currently travelling on, always travelling along the path of least resistance, believing that you are perfect just the way you are! So the more you try to change, the more opposition you will encounter. And you are up against your most powerful ally.

How has your Saboteur become so powerful? It's because your unconscious mind is like a wall that's been built up brick by brick, minute by minute, month by month, year after year – for decades. It doesn't matter if you're 15 years old, your unconscious mind has spent the entire time crafting a careful universe where every hope, dream, desire, pain, anguish, and fear have laid the foundations of your beliefs and values. These "beliefs" and "values" then become the solid bricks with which your unconscious mind builds the very wall that you will one day find yourself trapped inside.

And the older you get, the higher the wall; and the harder it becomes to change... well... anything! However, cheer up! Please, remember that no matter how difficult it might seem to overcome your beliefs and values, you do rule over your universe and your unconscious is always ready to replace tough old bricks for flexible new ones.

Within these pages I hope to show you how to change:

- **Your job**
- **Your weight**
- **Your income**
- **Your relationship status**
- **Your life!**

Why would your unconscious mind build this wall in the first place? Isn't it there to help? Of course it is! The fact is; your unconscious mind is simply trying to protect you from anything that challenges your status quo. It has created a world that is safe, that is placid, that is routine, and that is – above all else – comfortable. And it wants it to stay that way.

What's more, it thinks it knows best! So when you try something new, when you try to change, it will cause you to fail, swat you down and "sabotage" you because you can't possibly know all that it does about what's best for you.

This book is called *The Saboteur Within*. Why? Because that's what your unconscious mind is: a Saboteur Within. Its main job, all day long, every day – even when you're sleeping and unaware – is to "protect" you by building up that wall, that barrier, against anything new, unexpected or challenging.

And every time your conscious mind makes a stand, takes initiative and tries to overpower the unconscious – by joining a gym, going up for that promotion, asking someone out on a date – *The Saboteur Within* actively and openly begins to wage war against the new, the sudden, and the unexpected.

How? By sabotaging it, plain and simple. It does so by planting doubt in your mind, by reminding you of the sets of beliefs and values that were created by you when you were small, and your mind was wide open to suggestions back then.

Your unconscious will seek to reinforce this outdated and often-distorted image you have of yourself. These beliefs and values are so strong that in many cases you will fail to maintain the change that you so desperately desire. Why? Because that's just how the unconscious mind – *The Saboteur Within* – is.

What is the most powerful weapon in the unconscious mind's arsenal? Fear, plain and simple. All your unconscious has to do to sabotage any new or unique or challenging idea your conscious mind has, is to introduce a little healthy **fear** into the equation; the minute it does, most of us fold – just like that.

But fear represents unlimited opportunity. You live, for the most part, inside a very small box; we all do. That box contains all the routines, all the presumptions, all the assumptions, all the beliefs and values we have about who we are.

That box says:

- **"You're not handsome enough to ask her out."**
- **"You're not smart enough to get that new job."**

- **"If *you* got an 'A,' then the test must have been too simple."**
- **"Face it, you're fat and <u>you always will be!</u>"**

Who built the mental box that holds you back? You did, of course; or, more specifically, your unconscious mind did to keep you safe and away from danger. What's outside the box? The unknown, and your unconscious thinks that it's better for you to stay with everything that you know; even if it's an abusive relationship with someone or with yourself, via drugs, alcohol, smoking, obesity, etc, because you know what they are and you can be comfortable within your uncomfortableness. Even if your situation is very obviously limiting, it is the known and familiar, and that is what your unconscious has been told to do, keep you safe and away from the unknown (danger) at all costs. It is your fear of the unknown that will hold you prisoner.

A friend of mine called Stuart is a district judge and he told me about a woman who, after twenty years of marriage, filed for divorce. The woman told Stuart, who was a young solicitor at the time, that her husband had beaten her up every Friday night since they first got married. She said that he would return from the pub and promptly attack her. Stuart said that she had an unquestionable reason for divorcing him, but the woman said that that wasn't the reason for her seeking a divorce. Believe it or not, what had triggered her into taking action was the fact that "recently he has started going out on a Saturday night and giving me the same treatment when he comes home and that won't do at all!"

The Friday night beatings were known and part of a familiar pattern, something she had learned to live with. The Saturday night beatings were different and a challenge to the status quo, finally bringing her out of her comfort zone. In the chaos and confusion that was created by this change, she found the wherewithal to make a positive transformation in her life and was able to access the many more, infinite possibilities that existed outside of her abusive marriage. If only that lady knew what else is outside the box, she could have saved herself years and years of pain and misery. Some people would sooner die than change.

Opportunity, and lots of it, is just around the next bend if you are willing to go beyond your comfort zone? The more you step outside the box, the more fear you face, the more opportunity you will encounter – and the more likely you'll be to live the life you've always dreamed of!

This book is going to show you how to break out of your box, to tear down those walls, and to conquer the fear that's been holding you back. So far you've been outnumbered. The **conscious mind** is the tip of the iceberg; it accounts for about 5% of your daily thoughts. The other 95%? That's the entire **unconscious mind**; that's all you hear, all day long, telling you "no" instead of "yes" and "don't" instead of "do."

To date you have been powerfully outnumbered, but no more. You will, by the end of this book, realise that knowing and understanding your problems doesn't change anything. Only through **harnessing the power of the unconscious mind** will you take control of your life. Every lesson you learn will be another step out of the box the unconscious has built for you every day since you were born.

Every page you read will help you take control back; control of your body, your mind, your soul… your very life. It may be challenging, but I promise you this: it *will* be **simple**. The good news is that all the tools you need to live the life of your dreams are already in your possession. The better news is, this book will help you find them and then by learning to use them, will fully equip you to deal with your inner Saboteur.

∽

Chapter 1

Your Unconscious Mind, the Saboteur Within
"He who conquers others is strong; He who conquers
himself is mighty""

Lao Tzu

Imagine your mind as an iceberg.

The **<u>conscious</u>** thoughts you have all day, those "I must remember to pay that bill" or "Can I afford that holiday?" or "Does the new accounts manager fancy me?" everyday thoughts, represent the mere tip of the iceberg; your **<u>unconscious</u>** thoughts, beliefs, values, structures – tens of thousands of them every day – represent everything else that lies just below the water's surface.

In short, the unconscious mind is not playing fair!

For every conscious thought you have about changing your world, there are literally tens of thousands of hidden thoughts. Those 'hidden' thoughts are made up of unconscious beliefs, ideas and concepts, which run silently in the background out of your awareness. Some will be undermining and contradicting your conscious thoughts without you even noticing.

Picture a salmon swimming upstream, fighting the current every step or, in this case, every "stroke" – of the way.

Although thousands of salmon make the trip back to their breeding grounds every year, only a few actually survive the constant struggle to fight that all-too-powerful current. So, when an idea spawns inside your mind, it has to overcome lots of obstacles and is constantly swimming against the known, or the tide of opposing thoughts inside your mind, hence change seems difficult.

Well, that's what change is like. When you try to lose weight, go back to school, stop smoking, try for that promotion, ask for that pay rise, join that gym, or simply take a different route home from work (just try it some time), your conscious mind is literally **swimming upstream** against not just thousands, but tens of thousands of unconscious thoughts telling it, warning it, screaming at it to, "Turn around, go back, this is the wrong way, you don't belong here!"

∽

Why TRUE Change is So Difficult.

*"If you want to make enemies, try to **change** something."*
Woodrow T Wilson

If you'll recall from this book's introduction, your unconscious mind likes things just the way they are. So when it prevents change, it really believes that it's doing so for your own good.

Consciously you decide that you want to get slim and shed those extra pounds, at the very same time your unconscious is thinking:

*"Why do you want to lose weight? You're perfectly healthy the way you are. After all, your mother was eighty years old and **she** was fat. Your husband will become jealous if you start to lose weight and that will cause rows. He will be angry and jealous."*

2

"Why do you want that new job?" it thinks. *"Things are going just fine the way they are. At least I know where everything is here. Nobody will like me there. What if I can't do what they want?"*

"Why do you need a new boyfriend?" it thinks. *"We're just fine on our own! The first relationship was very painful so the next one will be worse. He will probably cheat on you anyway! My parents wouldn't approve."*

Change is a threat to the unconscious mind; not because it doesn't want what's best for you, but because it thinks it already *knows* what's best for you. That's because despite its sophistication and abundance of tens of thousands of thoughts per day, the unconscious mind is basically driven by emotions and it's probably easier to imagine it as an infant or young five -year-old.

That's about the age that you begin to learn about logic and your emotional mind is encouraged to become a rational one. Then the conscious mind begins its age-old struggle to try to retain some semblance of control over your life and how to live it. You will understand this even more as you venture further through the book.

It's relatively easy to "try" and change. How often have we gone out and bought the gym membership, splurged on a new suit, to meet with the boss and ask for a pay rise, bought all the healthy food at the supermarket or joined the online dating site looking for love? And we all start with great hopes and even greater expectations.

But fast forward a week or two and chances are we've stopped going to the gym, never asked for that pay rise, new job or promotion, the "good food" still stacked at the back in the fridge, has gone off – we haven't even touched it – and we never followed through on any of those promising leads from the dating site.

Why? Why is change – true change – so hard? Think about the last workshop, seminar, conference or self-help group you went to. It was all very encouraging, very inspiring, all very simple – and all done with a nice cup of tea.

You paid your money, walked in amongst like-minded people such as yourself, listened to an inspiring speech from someone who'd "made it" and then, walked out with a handful of books, tapes, CDs and DVDs and… then what happened?

What happened is that you barely cracked the self-help workbook, listened to half of the CD and used the DVD case to prop up the bookcase in your bedroom! That's because the instructor had no chance of breaking through that protective wall that's been built up by your unconscious mind for years and years, for decades and decades, in fact.

One two-hour conference, one rousing speech, a few minutes of inspirational quotes aren't going to be able to infiltrate the control held by the Saboteur Within; nope, that's a job that only YOU can pull off!

The minute you tried to be happier, think more positively, eat more healthily, or simply live better – **the very moment you tried to change** – your Saboteur sensed that change was in the air and started whispering lots of subtle scary thoughts in an effort to keep you 'safe' and well within your comfort zone, as far away as possible from the unknown.

Your conscious mind tried; it tried to get you to change. It led you to pay for that seminar, Google the address, drive straight there, even get there early and find the best seat in the house; you did all those things consciously, of your own free will. It helped you sit there and listen and learn and hope and feel and emote and try; and you tried so hard, and the fact that you were 'trying' is actually the root of the problem.

Let me explain a little more about the word "try". It is a direct command to your unconscious mind that what you have set out to achieve is way too difficult/complicated/ challenging and you are going to fail. How many times have you used the word 'try' when you were already thinking 'no, it's not going to happen.'? Have you ever heard yourself saying 'I'll *try* and get that report written this afternoon', 'I'll *try* and make it to your party', and 'I'm going to *try* to go running every day.'

Master Yoda said it best, when young Luke Skywalker was failing to use the force; Yoda said, "Do or do not... there is no try". The minute you tried implementing some of that change, your unconscious began whispering in your ear, telling you the effort wasn't worth it, that the CD was hooey, that the instructor didn't know what he was talking about. He made you feel uncomfortable, that you don't need to change – you just need to **keep the status quo**.

Your conscious mind was overwhelmed and drowned out, even as it yelled, "The status quo isn't working anymore!"

∾

Is Your Saboteur Within Making You Fall Asleep at the Wheel?

"When one realises
one is asleep,
at that moment
one is already half-awake"

P. D. Ouspensky

Have you ever fallen asleep at the wheel, only to wake up moments before a jarring collision when your tyres bumped against the curb or ran over the cat's eyes? You have probably experienced the feeling of "falling asleep at the wheel" even when you're *not* driving.

In fact we can fall asleep while standing up in many areas of our lives. It's easy to sleepwalk through our family life, for instance, settling into a routine of patterns and habits that often make us feel disconnected from our loved ones.

In romantic relationships we can find ourselves just going through the motions, wanting to change or improve things, but falling asleep again at the wheel and letting the relationship run its course under its own steam – for better or worse.

Recently I started falling asleep at the wheel with one of my businesses. It was running fine and very profitably, and it seemed like a good time to leave it in the hands of some very qualified people I thought I could trust. Big mistake as almost immediately I started to hear grumblings – from customers, employees, the bank, and the like.

That certainly woke me up in a hurry! But what stung even more was not just the money I lost while I was away; but what it would take to wrestle back control of my own business from those I had put in charge, even though it was for a relatively short time.

As you might imagine, at first, I was very upset by the situation I found myself in, but before long I soon began to appreciate the valuable lesson I learned. Yes, it cost me a great deal but getting that "wakeup call" was what it took for me to take a second, even a third look at the business and put myself back in the driving seat. Suddenly the business was "mine" again. I was no longer a sleepy passenger, instead, very much awake – and in control.

I was puzzled; when a few months later I began to feel myself starting to doze again and something definitely didn't feel right. After much soul searching and reflection, I realized that this particular business no longer felt in line with my true purpose in life. Sure, I could have forced myself to continue down that same road. The money was good, but my soul was pulling me in a new direction. So I passed the business on to a guy who had a real passion for it, and that is the point that I really began to concentrate on making sure I was working with purpose. As a result of this newfound focus, the seeds of life as a hypnotist, therapist, and coach began to germinate for me.

How about you? Are you in control at the moment? Not just of your company, but of your life? Are your relationships all they can be? Is work going as well as it could? Do you feel as good as you could? Examine your answers again after you have gone through the exercises in this book and then see how you feel. There is a powerful force at work, which could be derailing your life, even as you go about it with the best of intentions.

The worst part is; it's an inside job!

By putting your hands back on the wheel, you might momentarily think that you can "snap out of it" and steer your life in the right direction. But the truth is that all change, behavior and learning happen at a **below conscious level**, so if you have conflicting views on the next stage in your life, then you can bet your last penny that your plans will be sabotaged.

∽

Questions to ask to check if you are "Off Course"

I promised you an antidote to the Saboteur Within; some action steps you can take to help steer your life back on track, grab the wheel and make sure that this time, this one time, true change can happen – and will last – because you finally know the true source of what tripped you up all those other times: your **unconscious mind**.

The strongest tool the Saboteur Within uses against you is your ignorance. I don't mean that you're stupid, far from it. By ignorance I mean, quite literally, you are – or, at least, were – ignorant of the power that the unconscious mind has over you.

But no more, by reading and engaging with the principles in this book you can learn the power of the Saboteur Within, and fully engage with the powerful resource that lies within you. Beginning to question the influence your unconscious has, then, gradually at first, step-by-step, question-by-question, take back control of your life creating more empowering beliefs that your **unconscious mind** can uphold for you.

For the mathematicians amongst us, the 5%/95% rule is another way of looking at life. 5% you are conscious of and 95% goes on around you at a below conscious level.

Let's take a new relationship for example: You've just met and your new partner is everything that you could ever have wished for. That is your 100% initial input.

Over time you can begin to stop noticing the wonderful things that makes your relationship with your partner so special (the 95%) and, instead, focus on the things your partner does that wind you up! (The 5%)

You could transform your relationship right now just by focusing your attention on what is good about your partner and continuing that approach over the next month or so and notice the difference. You get what you focus on.

The first step is to question; question everything! The next time you pull into a fast-food restaurant two days after you start your diet, don't just order the special and supersize it **without thinking**.

Instead, **ask yourself: "Am I physically hungry?"** It could be that you only just ate half a supermarket and you really aren't hungry. Instead, maybe you're thirsty and need a glass of water. Or maybe you're lonely, sad, upset, or emotionally empty, so your unconscious is actually trying to satisfy these feelings the only way it knows how: with food, drugs and external stimulants! If you begin to **think** about what you truly want and how you can get it, then you engage your unconscious as a trusty servant. If however you continue to stay in the same loop of feeling unhappy, angry, or sad and attempting to make yourself feel better with food, alcohol, or prescription drugs, then the downward spiral will continue and change will feel even more difficult!

The next time you stand up from your desk and head straight past your manager's office instead of asking for that big pay rise like you'd planned, ask yourself what blew you off course.

Specifically, here is a train of thought I would encourage you to use: **The Outcome Frame**.

The Outcome Frame allows you to clearly let your unconscious mind know what you want to achieve, what that will do for you and the resources that you require to accomplish this. Think about this for a moment: let's say you are meeting up with a friend this weekend and you haven't set an outcome for the day.

Well, then it's very probable that they don't have an outcome either, or that your friend has a set outcome and will have you doing something for them. Sometimes this is fine and dandy but other times your unconscious can access emotions that seem right at the time, for example; you're being used or your friend doesn't value you, but that's your Saboteur aiming to ruin your relationship. That's why I encourage you to step up and take responsibility for setting a good outcome for yourself. A lot of people either bite the bullet and just put up with their time being used by others, or you can get angry and upset and never see your friend again! Not a very adult approach to life, is it?

OOOOPs! The truth of the matter is you did it to yourself. How? Well, by not setting The Outcome Frame, you set yourself up for disappointment – and that is exactly what you got! An Outcome Frame allows you to tap into the power of your conscious mind to give your day, or meeting, or outing, or lunch, or gym session "guardrails" to combat the power of the unconscious mind.

By creating specific goals for yourself – times, dates, durations, weights, schedules, etc. – you are consciously driving and in control of your life, but if you find yourself consistently sabotaging your set goals, then you have unconscious goals that are in conflict and they will beat you, every time. By using the exercises in this book you will be able to uncover your unconscious goals and get fully aligned with your life purpose.

I can't begin to tell you, when I have my business consultant's hat on, how many people in companies fail to set an outcome frame for their meetings. They come together, talk for the sake of talking, and there's no true outcome, so nothing gets decided upon. What happens at that point is that people get frustrated, which then spirals on to the next meeting and around the roundabout we go. In fact, some companies have been doing this for years – and many still do!

Avoid going around your own personal "roundabout" by setting an outcome frame for your daily schedule. If your daily schedule still seems to become undone, even though it has been written out on tablets of stone, then my friend the Saboteur is within your organisation, so give me a call and let's see what can be done. The basic rule of thumb is;

"If you've used measurements, systems and procedures to fix the problem and it's still a problem, then it's emotional. Someone within your organisation is benefiting by it failing." Please read "The Prince" by Niccolò Machiavelli. It's a short story and very aptly and concisely looks at the truth and its considerations, reference politics and ethics. The former I confess to know little about, the latter I aim to live by.

Failure: *There is No Such Thing as Failure, Only Feedback (So take the feedback from what you have been – and are doing – and do something different!)*

Nobody ever became a beached whale over night!

What's more common is to wake up one morning, glance at the mirror – often in shock! – And ask ourselves:

- **"Where did these extra 30 pounds come from?"**
- **"Why am I still in this dead end job?"**
- **"Why am I still in this crummy flat?"**
- **"Why am I still smoking all these years later?"**
- **"Why am I still living alone, <u>all these years later</u>?"**

Chapter 2

The 8 Rules of the Saboteur Within
"It's not wise to violate rules until you know how
to observe them."

T. S. Eliot

By now, in our discussion of the unconscious mind, you're probably feeling as if the "Saboteur Within" is downright unstoppable. I won't lie; true change can be very, very difficult unless you can engage the help of your Saboteur. In this next section I am going to arm you with eight powerful tools – I call them "rules" – that will give you a new understanding of, and mastery over, the unconscious mind:

ᖇ

Rule # 1 of the Saboteur Within

Thoughts = Physical Reaction

Mary was a seventy two year old woman who initially came to visit me because she had been experiencing chest pains. Apparently, this was nothing new for Mary. During our initial consultation, she shared with me that she had experienced chest pains as far back as she could remember.

When I asked Mary what she'd done in the past to alleviate her symptoms, she told me that she had taken medication for many years and sometimes the pain would ease a little and yet no matter what she took, or how often or when, the pain was always there. She confessed that she "never felt any freedom from the pain within her" and that she literally "couldn't take it anymore." She wanted to find some relief – at last.

As Mary sat in front of me for the first time that day, I thought I would use hypnosis and regress her to see where some of these physical ills might be stemming from. Hypnosis allows the client to deeply relax, whilst accessing a heightened state of awareness and communicate with their unconscious mind to work through their issues. In my experience, someone who's had chronic pain for as long as they can remember is usually displaying some physical reaction to strong emotions.

I decided to regress Mary ten years at a time. Each decade I asked Mary, "What can you see and sense?"

Each time Mary replied, "Nothing; it is all black." Each time I would say "Wonderful, Mary" and continue the regression.

I eventually regressed Mary all the way back to her wedding day, over five decades earlier. In my naiveté I had assumed that the day she got married must have been a happy day for Mary. However, when I asked what she was "experiencing" Mary replied, "Everything was black."

This time, however, I noted some serious nonverbal expressions accompanying her response. Her face was contorted a little and she felt that there was something within her she was not happy with. When I asked her about this, Mary said she "wasn't sure" what this negative feeling was about.

Eventually I got Mary to open up, not just about her wedding and why it was causing her "pain". Initially she was unable to express what she felt verbally, but by telling her what I was observing in her non-verbals, (facial expression, body posture etc) we began to explore the suffering she had experienced not just on her wedding day, but throughout her entire marriage, and how it had contributed to her nearly lifelong chest pains.

It eventually transpired that back in the time when Mary got married, your husband was legally allowed to rape you. In other words, even if a wife said "No" to sex, because she was legally married her husband couldn't be accused of raping her – even if he forced her to have sex against her will.

This experience had been horrific for Mary and had had an effect on her life from that day forward. Mary felt that she had never truly made love, but only "had sex" at her husband's will. Being a young woman at the time of her marriage and uninitiated in the "birds and the bees," Mary did not understand what was happening to her. She never associated sex with pleasure, or even with love or affection; all she could associate with this feeling was the pain.

If Mary and her husband went out for the evening when they were young and her husband had had a couple of drinks, she would notice that twinkle in his eye, which meant that they were going to have sex. Initially, Mary would feign a headache. This never worked, though, as he would still insist on forcing himself upon her and it would hurt Mary considerably. She never experienced any physical pleasure from the "act" and foreplay was something that you did on a Sunday night with friends in a game of cribbage.

Over the years the pain Mary experienced below her waist during intercourse quickly developed into chest pain. Amazingly, chest pain worked; it worked so well she would get out of breath and feel like she was going to die. The pain was so intense that her husband would leave her alone.

Now, many years later, even though Mary and her husband were now both in their 70's and sex had not been in the cards for a long, long time the physical reaction was still present. She couldn't actually allow herself to let her hair down and experience fun.

Here we have the unconscious mind at work, doing what it does best: turning thoughts into physical reactions. In Mary's case, she was associating sex with pain. Consciously, she could not say that to her husband as at that time he could beat her and still have sex; legally. So her unconscious mind designed a wonderful way of looking after the self at the expense of a lifetime devoid of fun, laughter, and sexual enjoyment.

The initial feelings that the client had were now locked inside her mind and had made her a prisoner. I now had to guide her back to that painful time in her life and allow her to let go of the negative emotions she'd learned to associate with sex and thus release the pain from her chest.

I had a hunch that Mary's feelings about sex had imprinted long before she met her husband, let alone married him. I decided that since most life imprints are developed by the age of five or six, it would be more feasible to begin at the beginning of Mary's life and bring her forward.

I said, "Right, Mary, in a moment I am going to ask you to close your eyes and ask you to wander back to a particular time and place inside your mind. As I count back from 5 to 1, I would like you to have the sensation of being born. Because you were born and the evidence is right here in front of me now 4, 3, 2, 1.... That's right and you are back there now and you are just being born. Now, Mary, tell me what do you see? How do you feel? And, what can you hear?"

At that moment Mary sobbed and wailed like a stricken animal. I asked, "Mary, what are you doing inside your mind, right now?"

She answered, "I can see my mother!"

I said, "Wonderful! What's happening now?"

Mary answered, "She's dying!" That's right; Mary's mother had died during childbirth and Mary had repressed the memory, but that hadn't prevented her from carrying around the pain and guilt and sadness for the rest of her life. And right there and then, some 72 years after her own birth, Mary mourned the death of her mother and the pain vanished. She had carried it all those years, never consciously knowing that there was something so distressing and emotional, she could never have dealt with back then.

This subsequently affected Mary's relationship with her husband, as the thought of sex and pregnancy also had connections with an insurmountable fear of pain and death. During regression therapy, Mary released the pain from her body.

As you can see, Mary wasn't pretending to be in pain, but nor did she know what the cause of her pain was. Yes, consciously she understood that her mother had died whilst giving her life, but where did the pain come from? The family who looked after her and brought her up could have transferred the pain. When she first started playing with other children, who had mums, the pain of being without her mum or being different could have been imprinted deep inside her mind, or as Karl Jung put it her "Personal Unconscious". We could speculate all day, but let me simply state that by allowing Mary's unconscious mind to access the emotions that were locked up back then, she was able to release the pain from her system. Mary fed back to me a few weeks later that she had never genuinely experienced happiness in her life and now she felt as though a great weight had been lifted from her. Mary's Saboteur had maintained her sadness and fear as it was the routine she had been born into. Thankfully she was now fully able to experience true happiness and joy.

∽

Rule # 2 of the Saboteur Within:

Expectation = Realisation

A mother called my office one day, and asked if I could work with her daughter. She was seven years old, a tiny little girl. Unfortunately, she was in a great deal of pain and could not walk without the aid of crutches.

The specialists had examined her and found that, since she was so small, a problem in the muscle and bone development of her feet was creating all the pain. There was no need for an operation, however, as by the time she was 12 years old she would have grown sufficiently and there would be no long-term problems.

Since I knew I was going to visit a child, I took a teddy bear with me. Sometimes, I've found, it's easier for children to speak to toys and animals. Her mother and I were both concerned with the fact that Sarah could not play and interact with her friends as she would like to. We were worried about the long-term problems that this isolation could create in her personal development.

I asked mom to leave Sarah and I and go into the other room. I did this as, in my experience, it is often impossible for young children to express themselves fully when their parents are around, because they will seek approval of what they say and may be reluctant to be open and honest about what they are experiencing. Once we were alone, I asked Sarah if she liked teddy and she smiled and said, "Yes." I then told Sarah that Teddy would like to come and live with her and she was very happy about this idea. I went on to tell Sarah that Teddy was very excited about moving in with her. However, there was a drawback; Teddy would only feel happy if older people who could keep him safe were looking after him.

Next, I covered teddy's ears so that he couldn't "hear" and asked Sarah if she could pretend to be 13 years old, of course we wouldn't tell teddy. It would be our little secret. She smiled and said, "Yes." So, I told Teddy that even though I would miss him, Sarah would really be able to look after him and Sarah walked straight across the room and picked up Teddy. I asked her what she liked most about being 13 and she excitedly said, "Staying up late and wearing mummy's make-up!"

I told her to go and show mummy her new teddy. Sarah walked straight out of the room to tell mum and, seeing her daughter walking without pain made Sarah's mother cry.

"You are walking," she said, and Sarah looked at her with an "of course I am" look on her face.

Then she said, "I am a big girl now." The rest is history; Sarah walked pain-free from that day forward and proved our second rule of the Saboteur Within: expectation = realization. In other words, if you expect something to happen – it will.

You're probably thinking that this is preposterous, but there are many examples of the placebo verses nocebo effects. In 1952 Dr. Albert Mason was using hypnosis to treat a 15-year-old boy's warts. Many doctors had successfully used hypnosis in the treatment of warts and Mason was very good at it. This time, however, the boy was covered from head to toe and his skin looked like cracked leather.

Dr. Mason was to create a medical sensation with this patient, because one week after his session the boy returned and his arm, which is the part of his body Dr. Mason had suggested to get well, was perfectly healthy and clear. After a few more sessions the boy's skin totally cleared up and he went on to lead a normal life.

How did it make medical history? Well, the boy was suffering from a lethal genetic disease called congenital ichthyosis and Dr. Mason hadn't prescribed any drugs. He only used hypnosis to reverse all of the boy's symptoms. At the time of working with the boy, he was totally unaware that the condition was incurable.

When Dr. Mason wrote about his startling treatment for ichthyosis in the British Medical Journal in 1952, his article created a sensation. Dr. Mason became a magnet for patients suffering from the rare, lethal disease that no one before had ever cured.

Dr. Mason attempted to help other ichthyosis patients, but was never able to replicate the results he had with the young boy. Now that he knew that the disease was incurable, his own belief was weakened, and the patient could unconsciously pick up on Dr. Mason's doubt.

Mason Quote:

"I had a mother who was very ill when I was a child, and so the need to cure was really linked to my relationship to an ill mother and that's just what you need to be a hypnotist. You need a kind of *furor therapeutica*. The congenital case I cured, I'm sure, needed to be cured as much as I needed to cure him and something strange happened. After that case, half a dozen ichthyotics came to see me and I never cured another one. By that time I knew it was incurable, so, there was the difference, that kind of conviction I had that I could cure him was no longer there. So that was really my history and how I became an analyst."

I always tell therapists and coaches in my trainings that they must believe in the client's ability to create a miracle. You see; if your coach doubts their ability to help you or your ability to help yourself, either way you are doomed to fail. On the other hand if your coach, therapist, doctor, mum, or dad let go of their ego and has absolute faith in you, then miracles can and do happen.

If you spend all your time expecting to be poor, you will be poor; expecting to be unloved, you will be. The unconscious mind will construct an "I am" story for you and every belief and value you have will go to support that particular story. The question is does your story help you and support you or not?

Sarah and her mother hadn't expected to be pain-free until she was older. Therefore, Sarah was fully prepared to live with excruciating pain, isolation and lack of socialisation with her peers. She "expected," and so her expectations were "realised."

Here I used the rule to the full. Sarah's mum believed the specialists, Sarah believed her mum. So when the specialist said she would be in pain until she is 13, her problem fitted the expected criteria and the brain and nervous system responded accordingly. So I had to give Sarah another expected state of mind, which was one of already being **13 years old**.

Sarah's mind already knew on an unconscious level that at 13 there would be no pain in her feet and she would be living a normal life. So by creating the scenario that she was already 13, I had the client create the **expectation** and thus the **realisation** of a healthy physical pain free life. What happens when the child realises that she is not 13 years old? Nothing at all because she has made a change on an unconscious level, which will run and run until a better update overrides the message.

This technique works well with anxiety, because in order to be anxious about anything, your mind has to expect a problem in a future event. Have you ever been invited to a party and told yourself "it will be rubbish", and you go anyway and guess what? It was rubbish! It happened exactly the way you thought it would be. Why? Because **expectations lead to realisations**!

The same can be said on the positive side, where people have a strong belief that they deserve to succeed in whatever endeavor they have chosen to undertake. They don't fail because they don't expect to fail; they succeed because they expect to succeed. As we move further through the book there are some exercises that should help you to get to grips with this.

Rule # 3 of the Saboteur Within:

Imagination is More Powerful Than Knowledge

No matter how unreasonable a human being's beliefs or superstitions are, if they imagine them to be true – they are true; at least for them. As we continue through the book, I will show you many examples of clients who, even though they have a detailed knowledge of what caused or is causing their problem, they are unable to be set free until they engage with their imagination.

When Simon came in to my office wanting to stop smoking, I was very interested in the fact that every ten seconds or so he rubbed his nose. Simon went on to explain that, after many tests, he had been found to be allergic to nicotine and that was why he needed to stop smoking.

Simon had sought out knowledge for his bizarre "nose rubbing" behaviour and so here he was ready to work with hypnotherapy to overcome his cigarette addiction. As Simon sailed into a relaxing trance, I decided it would be fun to test out the 'diagnosis' of nicotine addiction. I worked with his unconscious to use the part of his mind that was driving his smoking habit and align it with the part of him that was making his nose sore.

I then asked his unconscious mind to find brand new ways of allowing these reliable behaviours to support Simon in his life moving forwards.

The whole session lasted about an hour and when Simon opened his eyes we chatted about this and that for twenty minutes and he left. The next day Simon's wife telephoned to thank me because Simon hadn't touched his nose once since leaving me and he hadn't even mentioned cigarettes. You see I had worked with the fact that Simon believed, because of the information he had been given by 'experts', that by stopping smoking his nose would no longer be sore and he would therefore stop touching it. I decided to work in the opposite way and by stopping him touching his nose using light trance, then he would stop smoking. The logic is the same except for one thing - if Simon was truly "allergic to nicotine" as the specialists had told him, then it would have taken a few weeks for his system to be clear of all traces of nicotine. Consequently it would also have taken a few weeks for the irritation in his nose to subside, not simply forgetting all about it one hour after a conversation with me.

I was recently a keynote speaker at a workshop for cancer patients in Manchester, England, and at the end of the session I agreed to give a demonstration of how powerful the imagination is. I asked for volunteers with a fear of heights to come forward. I got eight volunteers to stand in a line. Working with one person at a time, it took less than seven minutes to change their negative imagination into a positive one.

When you ask someone with a height phobia to imagine that they are on the 36th floor of a skyscraper, three feet from the patio door, and that the balcony outside has no railings, just a long drop straight down to the busy street below, it's amazing just how their mind allows them to access that situation. Immediately the body stiffens, heart rate increases, their hands become clammy, sweat pops out on the brow, their throat becomes very dry, and they look absolutely petrified!

What a brilliant use of your mind! How else to explain the sudden visualisation these people experience to make them physically and emotionally terrified; even when they know that they're standing, safely, on the ground! Now, I can't walk from the living room to the kitchen without forgetting what I went in there for and yet these guys can, instantly and vividly, remember every single detail of how to be scared and all of the subsequent behaviour that specific fear creates for them. It happens automatically, they don't have to think about it, just like sneezing, you don't have to remember how to do it or plan it, it just happens.

Do you know what fear is? Fear means **F**alse **E**vidence **A**ppearing **R**eal. With a phobia, however, the fear *is* genuine to the client. They honestly believe in their imagination that they are no longer standing in a room being watched by sixty other people. In their minds, they are actually in that skyscraper and everyone else watching can see, quite clearly, by the panic on their faces and the sweat on their brows that they are responding as if it were real.

When you hold that fear inside your mind, the picture is very strong and the feeling is very real. In order to separate the picture from the feeling, I have the client sing a silly song inside their mind and, all the while, walking forward. At the same time I tell them that I have a red cloak that is allowing me to fly and I lend them a spare red cape so that they can fly with me too.

Then we "fly" in their imagination to the 50th floor and wave across to the spectators in the other buildings. I ask the client to count how many people they can see smiling and waving back at them, all the while continuing to have them sing their silly song, something like, "The sun has got his hat on". This also has the desired effect of having them mix a fun chemical within their hypothalamus whilst thinking about a context which formerly scared the bejesus out of them! Then we come back to land on the 34th floor and they are safe in the room again.

Next, I ask them to open their eyes, see me standing there three steps away from them and walk toward me. Now, I ask them what they can hear. When they reply with "a silly song," I know that **their fear has been conquered**. The "silly song" and the feel good chemicals that accompany it have overridden the original voice that was running in their mind, making it feel comfortable for them. It probably seems too quick and easy, but so long as I am able to make the client do some fun, crazy stuff, then I am helping them to change their internal chemical response to the external stimulus. The mind generalises the new stimulus response automatically as long as there is enough fun attached to it!

The entire technique took less than fifteen minutes and by the time I got to volunteer number eight, his mind had already piggy backed on the technique I'd used with the others, so I quite literally patted him on the back and congratulated him for having done a marvellous job! He smiled, knowing his fear had left him.

It was interesting to note that only one of the clients, Sally, doubted what she had done that day. A couple of months later she emailed me to inform me that she had just been to Paris, and what's more she'd gone **up the Eiffel Tower**. It wasn't until she came down that she realised she had actually been up there, all the way to the top, without fear and terror. You see once the imagination has been given a more useful outcome, it will always choose the best option available, given the resources on hand at the time.

If you were to consider that you are observing the world and your observations appear on a large screen in front of you, the challenge then is to adjust the settings on your screen until it feels better.

Height phobia example: In order to have a height phobia you have to drop your screen on the floor and imagine that you are standing on the edge of an abyss, which you are about to fall into! Voilà, you have the structure of a height phobia. Now to fix it all you have to do is fill the void full of stuff, thoughts, imaginary concrete, anything that you want, until it's absolutely full to the top, and then step on it to make sure that it's okay. Hey Presto! You have now cured a height phobia. There are lots and lots of ways to adjust your screen and thus adjust your life, so chase me up if you ever need a hand.

Rule # 4 of the Saboteur Within:

Opposing Ideas Cannot be Held Simultaneously

Jane was in her late 40's and her presenting problem was spondylitis. In other words, she could not lift her hands up above her chest because to do so would create excruciating pain. She had been subjected to all the x-rays and specialist tests, and she munched on pain killing pills daily. The problem began 25 years ago and started with a twinge in her neck that gradually got worse and worse.

When we started working together, I used some simple relaxation techniques and the client reported immediate relief from pain. I had her move her neck fully in all directions to see how it felt and she could lift her arms naturally. Jane left my clinic that day feeling very, very happy with herself.

However, that evening all was not well in the mind of Matt Hudson. I felt it was just too easy to solve Jane's problem and that we hadn't found the actual opposing belief that made Jane present with her pain in the first place.

If you put the book down for a moment and rub your hands together, you will create heat. The same can be said when you are holding opposing ideas.You will create a "friction" within the body and this, in itself, can cause pain or dis-ease. Even though we seemed to have solved Jane's pain, I thought one more session would be in order to get to what caused the pain in the first place.

About a week later Jane was back in to see me. When I asked her how she'd been feeling, Jane said that she had had a little twinge of pain since our last meeting, but that she'd remembered the technique I'd taught her, which was simply see the pain, notice what colour it is, and change the colour until it feels better. This method of visualisation allowed Jane to switch off the pain.

"Ah ha," I said, "I was right, because if we got the root of the problem, the pain would not have popped up again so soon, if at all."

Jane looked at me as if I might be a little crazy, personally the best look a client can give. It just says to me, "This isn't normal!"

I next asked Jane to sit back in the chair, close her eyes, and contemplate what started happening in her life 26 years ago when the pain first presented itself, that is still happening today.

What happened next defies belief and I can only tell you as I saw it: Jane's body went into full spasm. Seriously, you would think she was sitting in an electric chair. She was physically pained and I was elated.

"Yes!" I thought to myself. "Now we're getting somewhere!"

I asked her what was happening in her life back then just before the pain started. She said "I know it sounds silly, but..." "Hooray!" I thought, you see if someone begins with "This may sound crazy", or, "I know it sounds daft but..," they are telling you that there is a direct correlation between what they are saying and what has transpired: but they don't know how they can possibly be connected. She went on to tell me that her mother had become ill 26 years earlier. She had just got married and was starting a family. As a caring daughter, she would try her best to help her mum by popping around daily. At the same time, she had to look after her own family. Jane juggled this situation all on her own because her two sisters had exited stage, left and right, leaving Jane to do all of the caring for her mother.

Now, here are the conflicting beliefs that were originating in Jane's mind and presenting themselves as physical pain in Jane's body.

Belief: "I love my mother and I must always help my mother..."

The "must" (model operator of necessity) suggests that Jane has no say in the matter.

The "always" (Generalisation) means there has never, and will never, be a time when Jayne won't help her mother.

Conflicting Belief: "My sisters are single and they should help my mother as I have children and I have to be there for my children because I am a mother"

The "should," (model operator of necessity) suggests that the sisters are disobeying the family rule, because they aren't helping mother. This is all going on inside Jane's head by the way.

The "I am" (Identity Statement) Jane is viewing her sisters from the viewpoint of a mother, so as daughters they aren't doing what they are supposed to be doing.

Jane was experiencing a lot of guilt over these conflicting emotions; guilt about not being there for her mother, because when she was with her mother she should be caring for her children, and guilt about caring for her own children when she should be caring for her mother. Underneath Jane's guilt was a lovely heap of anger, which was quietly bubbling away deep beneath the surface. The feelings presented themselves as pain so Jane's health was sabotaged, sacrificed if you will, in order to maintain the integrity of Jane's whole system. Jane becoming ill would mean that her sisters would have to step in to help out and she could exonerate the guilt and anger she felt without having to have a blazing row with her sisters, because that would upset mum if she found out.

When Jane had been given the chance to fully evaluate her beliefs by writing them down and noticing which ones were helping her and which were sabotaging her, the pain left her body for good. She has since gone on to become a swimming instructor with a full range of body movements.

∽

Exercise

Think about your problem and sit for a while with a pen and paper, simply write
MY ...(Whatever the issue is)..................... means ....
Once you have written that statement, look at your meaning and follow up with
..... and that means...............
Write down that answer and again follow up with a further 5 or 6 x "and that means?"
For example, my frequent headaches means... I take lots of time off work
And that means...
I worry about my sick record at work
And that means...
I feel that my colleagues resent me
And that means...
I don't feel 'part of the gang'
And that means...
I feel lonely and isolated at work
And that means....
I feel very sad
And that means...
I want to work where I can feel happy and appreciated
Now put together your first statement with the last one...
My frequent headaches mean I want to work where I can feel happy and appreciated

Have a look at your answers; maybe get a friend or family member to work through it with you. You'll be surprised at what crazy nonsense some of your beliefs are founded on.

~

Rule # 5 of the Saboteur Within:

An Unconscious Idea Remains Fixed Until Replaced by a Better One

A woman named Susan had come to me to help her stop smoking, which fits really well alongside this rule. Susan was in her late 50`s and she had smoked for 40 years, 60 cigarettes a day, and worked in a bingo hall. I haven't been in a bingo hall for many years. I am assured, however, that nowadays they have very good extraction systems, but back then all was smog.

Susan desperately needed to stop smoking as her health was suffering badly due to bronchial problems. Consciously, she had tried to stop several times and failed every time. Why had she failed? Because just saying, "This will be good for me. I will be healthy," is not going to beat your Saboteur. Her Saboteur whispered temptingly, "Cigarettes help me to relax. I can't quit now". That might seem like a bit of an odd belief, but let me tell you how Susan's Saboteur came up with that, "Cigarettes help me to relax."

Susan's "origin story" about becoming a smoker is not so unique. When Susan first started smoking, she coughed and spluttered like most young people, but she "stuck at it" so that she could relax, mix with the other "big girls", and belong to the larger group. So after a week or so, Susan's unconscious mind – the Saboteur Within, remember – got the message that **cigarettes helped her to relax**.

Here we are now, 40 years down the line, and the client cannot convince her own mind that smoking isn't good for her! Even though the evidence to the contrary is compelling, to say the least. Her health has greatly deteriorated and still the unconscious message that "smoking is relaxing" remains fixed.

So many people visit hypnotists and therapists and expect them to stop them from smoking, but nobody ever "stopped" anybody from doing anything and, sometimes, even suggesting that some one "stop" something can encourage them to do more of the same. I couldn't "cure" Susan's addiction to nicotine; only she could. How? By taking on the Saboteur Within!

I started by asking Susan what she liked about the cigarettes. She said that they calmed her and made her feel relaxed. Then I pointed out that if you ever had an accident, the first thing the paramedics do is to put a mask on your face to give pure oxygen. The reason for this is because oxygen allows you to become calmer and more relaxed.

Yet there she was being able to puff on a cigarette, which contains smoke and nicotine, and actually convince herself into believing that she is becoming "calmer" as she smokes. I next said that since she had been able to rely for 40 years on the habit, wouldn't it be a good idea to utilise this reliability and have it do something else for her in return?

Now, I ask you, if you had a best friend who you could rely on for 40 years – night and day, rain or shine – and you came to meet a guy like me and I told you never to see that friend again and that friend had never done anything wrong, would you listen to me?

This is what many try to do when they want to quit smoking. They seek another external stimulus, a patch or a piece of gum to retain the internal stimulus that the mind can supply. Even if they understand that the unconscious mind is behind the reinforcement that smoking is "relaxing", they don't really appreciate the strength behind the behaviour. The Saboteur has immense capabilities. However, the same behaviour that made us do something bad can also help us do something good, so that when we have that strength move into a different area of our lives, we then have a good, solid resource with many years of trust behind it.

So when that strength is given a new role in our life it runs it effortlessly, allowing us to get on with the job of living. My job was to use Susan's strength and point it in a new direction; we needed to use her consistency and reliability for the purpose of something good, healthy and that would truly make her feel calm and relaxed.

We opted for helping Susan feel healthier, fitter, and stronger. Which were three ideas that Susan consciously could accept. Using "The 6 Step Reframe" (a simple NLP technique) I then helped Susan's mind to accept these thoughts unconsciously, thus overwriting the original imprint.

It takes 66 days to "make or break" a habit. I wonder if that's why a lot of advertisers give you a "free" trial, because they know that if you keep the product or service for 60 days or more, there is a huge likelihood that you will have come to rely on whatever it is they are selling you, because it has **actually become a habit**.

Using hypnosis, it's possible to take that 66-day period and condense it into a half-hour session. This isn't magical. It's just the way that your mind can distort time. You will have many everyday examples like; waiting for a bus, a train or an elevator, time can drag and a minute can seem like an hour. When you're having fun and enjoying yourself, hours can whizz by in seconds. I remember when I had a crash in my car. I could see the driver heading into the rear of my vehicle. I braced for impact and although it only took seconds, I thought that I had time to nip home, put on clean underwear, go to the movies, and then have lunch before getting back into the soon to be car crash! So time is up to you. Is it time for you to change now?

Almost a year went by before I heard from Susan. She had put away the money that she used to spend on cigarettes and used it to pay for her flight to Australia to see her sister, after not having visited her in 25 years! But that wasn't all. Susan told me that when she smoked she would do it in the garden shed, when her husband went out of the house. After our session, she would find herself nipping out into the garden shed without any cigarettes. She would stand laughing at herself, because her mind was still carrying her to her relaxation destination. ☺

It was amazing to see the progress. It was as though Susan had never ever smoked at all, let alone for 40 *long* years. If nicotine is supposedly as "addictive" as the pharmaceutical industry would have us believe, how then is it possible that a woman who has smoked 60 cigarettes a day for 40 years can quit after one hour and have no adverse effects to her health or any withdrawal symptoms?

I'll answer my own question: **An Unconscious Idea Remains Fixed Until Replaced by a Better One**. In other words, the power of the unconscious mind is so great that when it is presented with an alternative that is "better" than an original default setting – such as smoking is good for you – it can then use the same powerful force of the Saboteur Within to focus on the "better" idea and make it equally as strong. Many people will try this technique and it simply doesn't work. One of the reasons that they don't succeed is that they fail to access the same or better drivers than the original stimuli, so the internal chemicals don't switch. The best technique, and I've used it forever, is the 6 Step Reframe.There are plenty of examples of this NLP method all over the internet, or you can chase me up and I'll go through it with you on one of our training courses.

∽

Rule # 6 of the Saboteur Within:

Emotional Pains Can Create Physical Change

If you've ever doubted the power of the human mind, hear this: "In the twenty-first century it has been hypothesized that lifestyle-related disease will account for more than 70% of all disease; http://www.ncbi.nlm.nih.gov/pubmed/11519181

Case in point: Iris came to me with inflammation of the knee, which was so bad she had been put on a list for knee replacements.

Iris had worked as a cleaner for many years and her doctor had said that this problem was "to be expected" and had put it down to normal "wear and tear." She was 56 years old, a mother to four children, who had grown up and moved out of the family home leaving her alone with her husband.

Iris described to me how excruciating her pain was when walking and how the painkillers worked for a short time, but that now the pain seemed to be "constant." When asked if there were any times that she didn't feel pain, Iris immediately said, "NO!" After a bit of probing, however, we managed to discover that whilst reading her favorite Catherine Cookson books, Iris was actually able to relax enough to be pain free.

"So if you walked around reading Catherine Cookson all day, your knees would be okay?" I asked with a chuckle.

She smiled and said "If only," before breathing a deep, longing sigh.

Knowing that there was something sitting under the surface of her wistful answer, I asked, "What prevents you from doing what you want to do?"

Another sigh and then, "My husband..."

Iris then went on to explain that her husband was always ill and spent a lot of his time lying upstairs in bed. In fact, rather than be able to get up and walk downstairs to help himself, he would thump on the floor with a stick to summon her. A scowl flashed across her face for a second as Iris replayed the constant "thumping" sound to herself.

I asked, "What goes through your mind as you hear your master summoning you?"

She smiled, saying, "I couldn't possibly say it out loud."

As I'm sure you can guess, all was not well in this relationship. In fact, Iris was so locked into her pain that she would put her husband's meal on a tray and balance it on her knees as she shuffled up the stairs one at a time on her bottom.

She was very angry at having to be her husband's "servant," but she had no choice. They were too proud to ask for state help. Her husband's care was up to Iris. Well, in enters the Saboteur. You consciously do what you have to do because you don't want to upset the status quo, but your unconscious is listening to you when you are talking to yourself whilst in an emotional state.

So, in the case of Iris, if you didn't want to go upstairs but couldn't say "no" because you didn't want to upset anybody, what would you do?

This particular client had no conscious solution to: "If I can't walk up the stairs, he will have to come down!" But her unconscious mind sabotaged her health, so she was almost unable to walk and her husband had to come downstairs.

Now, if Iris had tried to do this consciously, she would have had to confront her husband and explain to him that she wasn't happy with the situation. It would have required a lot of courage and she just wanted an "easy" life, even though the one she had wasn't so easy either!

When this inner conflict was brought to the surface, I used hypnosis to relax Iris and utilised the information, which I had gleaned from our session within the trance.

Within a month of the session Iris, who had somehow found the nerve to explain to her husband that he "needed to take responsibility for his health and she wouldn't be up and down the stairs any more, as she wanted to be out and about, enjoying life", was able to go for long walks. This meant that her husband had to get out of bed, which he grudgingly did for the first couple of weeks and then his energy levels rose too, so that they got to actually spend good times together. 10 years later Iris has still had no recurrence of her knee problems and her husband has miraculously got "well" again!

Human beings are geared up to take the path of least resistance and illness can provide an easy ride for some people. A period of poor health can bring many secondary benefits for the patient. They don't have to do things for themselves, people around them will take care of their needs, they don't have to go to work and friends, and family will make a fuss and make them the centre of attention.

When Iris's husband was sick, she cared for him and ran around after him. Then Iris began taking less care of him and more care of herself. The benefits of coming downstairs and being well outweighed the benefits of lying upstairs and being unwell.

It all goes to show how intimately our minds and bodies are connected. When emotional pain is strong enough, it will translate into physical pain. The key is to know when a pain is truly physical, or coming from your mind. The minute Iris saw the connection between her knee pain and her husband's constant thumping, her mind awakened to the idea that it was her mind that was the cause of her pain, not her knees.

In July 2002 arthroscopic knee lavage or debridement was proven to be no better than placebo surgery in a randomised controlled trial. Basically, in a trial group of patients all expecting knee surgery, only half of the patients had the full operation whilst the other 50% simply received a small incision to make it appear that surgery had taken place, but they did not undergo an operation. The latter group faired as well as the group who had had the full operation!

When Fred the bank manager came he had been diagnosed with Helicobacter Pylori, a germ that lives in the

human stomach. It can lay dormant and cause no problems for many people, but for some with stomach ulcers,
it can create a big problem, which can be treated effectively with a course of antibiotics.

Fred had had several courses of various drugs and was
still suffering. The strange thing was that when he was at
home on Fridays and Saturdays he was okay, when he took
a two-week holiday abroad and ate foreign food, drank
lots of alcohol, he was okay, but as soon as he pointed towards the bank, his illness would flair up!

Fred's bank was being taken over by "money grabbing
ruthless executives, who don't care about my customers,
just profits!" he explained rather venomously. Fred had
worked for the bank for thirty years and he wasn't at all
happy at the way the new order of things was shaping up.
There would be many redundancies and "it's gutting me",
"tearing me apart", "it turns my stomach," the metaphors
flowed forth from Fred one after the other.

We worked on separating Fred from the bank as he was
actually mentally connected to everything that represented the bank, so every single thing that affected the bank's
status quo was affecting Fred.

Over several sessions Fred decided to take early retire-
ment and he reported to me that from the moment he decided to be free from the bank his stomach was calm and
still. Several years later, I still bump into Fred now and again.
He's still helping people and laments about how he could
see the writing on the wall for the banking crisis. Funnily
enough he has never had a recurrence of any kind of stomach ulcer and as he put it "I am a new man, since leaving
the bank."

Fred's pain was only active when he was at work, when
he returned home it subsided and it all began with the
change in the way in which his bank did business.

So have you had a change of management, business
direction, and organisational culture? Maybe sitting down
and separating what you do from who you are would be

a very good idea for you. Fred believed that he was the bank, but the bank is a thing not a human being.

To round off this section, let's take a closer look at what can lie behind ill health. Please remember no one is ill on purpose. I like to think of it this way, is it possible for two people who love each other to have a disagreement? The answer is yes, of course! Now if you consider your body is made up from 72 trillion individual cells, each with their own sense of purpose, is it, therefore, conceivable that there could be a dispute running between some of these individuals, so much so that they actually sabotage each other? Work through the exercise below, answering each question honestly to open up insights into the deeper meanings behind your ailments. Then, consider how you can encourage new meanings within yourself to align all of you in a common purpose.

Exercise

What does your ...(insert illness)........ mean to you?

What are the benefits of your .....(Insert illness)....?

What does your ......(insert illness)...... allow you to do?

What will you get if you do change?
What will you get if you don't change?
What won't you get if you do change?
What won't you get if you don't change?
Don't just rattle off a very surface, conscious answer, ask your friend to grill you. Remember your Saboteur will deliver the first few answers that you come up with, because your current condition might actually be serving a purpose....

∽

Rule # 7 of the Saboteur Within:

The More You Do It, The Easier "It" Gets

This rule is probably one of the easiest to adhere to, because once you accept a suggestion unconsciously, it makes it easier for additional suggestions to be accepted – and thus easier for you to act upon them. Even though I've said it's easy, there is a problem! You have to sit back, relax, and allow yourself permission to just be, calm, still, peaceful, tranquil, quiet.... That's right.... And for some that seems impossible, but it is achievable.

To give an example of this rule in effect, I would like to tell you about a woman named "Barbara," who I met while on holiday in Greece. She was a mother in her 40`s with two daughters and a loving husband. I was by the poolside and I noticed that Barbara seemed very uncomfortable near the water.

After a little pleasant chatting, I found out that when she was young she had been thrown into a pond by some older children and was terrified. Ever since then, Barbara had never ever learned to swim, because as she got older the suggestion that she "couldn't" swim became more and more powerful.

I asked if Barbara could drive a car and she said, "Yes, of course."

I said, "WOW, you manage to sit in a vehicle and drive. Do you have the radio on a lot of the time?" I enquired.

She said, "I do, yes."

I then said, "Well, I bet you can chat and listen to the radio at the same time as driving. Can you remember when you first started to drive how difficult it was, using your legs, switching gears, etc.?"

Barbara nodded, not quite sure where this was going. "And here you are today, an accomplished driver," I said.

"Well, swimming is a lot easier than driving. Did you know that?"

I then proceeded to build successive suggestions upon how competent Barbara was at being able to move her arms and legs on an unconscious level and thus drive a vehicle, and "being a woman" it was a very brave thing to do. Some times it's better to break rapport in order to get you into the right frame of mind and that last statement just does it nearly every time! ☺ Then I asked Barbara to step into the pool at the shallow end; she did. We then spent 30 minutes, chatting in the pool. The next day after breakfast our two families went to the beach and here Barbara began to learn to swim.

Within a couple of hours she had accomplished 20 yards of unbroken swimming. She was ecstatic. I had quite literally listened to her suggestion that she could not swim and replaced it with a suggestion that she "could learn" and that she was, in fact, **<u>open to learning</u>**.

This open suggestion leaves no conscious or unconscious defence, as everybody is open to learning. Now her unconscious mind would give less opposition to any subsequent suggestions of her becoming a competent swimmer.

How did I help Barbara to change?

- I watched the way she timidly approached the water to cool down from the sun, she was scared.
- I spoke to her from inside the pool, as she lay safe on the outside. Building rapport
- I directed the conversation to and around her driving, not commenting about the weather and usual holiday small talk. This causes a little confusion.
- I parallel the learning state of driving to swimming, after all, learning is learning.
- I tell her how brave she is to drive "being a woman." ☺
- When I ask her to step into the pool she is in a determined "I'll show you, you male chauvinist git!" state of mind.
- The internal chemistry is now one of purpose and not fear.
- Once in the pool, she practiced, I smiled, and we left her to it.
- By leaving her, she became even more intent on proving to me that she could do it.
- She went to bed and slept while her mind swam for many hours.
- She got up early, met us at breakfast, and asked if we would like to go to the beach to swim.
- The invite presupposed that Barbara was pretty confident that she was going to show me what she was made of!
- Result, a non-paying client gets a result she couldn't have dreamed about and I look like a bit of a male chauvinist git! All in all a good days work. ☺

∽

Exercise

1. Consider something that you currently can't do but would like to be able to do?
2. As you consider it, think about something that you currently do that is similar in process to that which you want to achieve.
3. You might want to get your best friend to give you a hand with this one. ☺
4. Continue to switch from step 1 and 2 inside your mind and give yourself permission to act as if it were possible.
5. The more energy you give to it being possible and already having an existing road map, which is similar to it, will accelerate your learning, so that you can attain your desired outcome more quickly.

∽

Rule # 8 of the Saboteur Within:

The More You Try, the Harder it Gets

Poor Tommy had insomnia. According to his mum, Tommy always wakes up about three in the morning. Tommy, now 11, goes to school and is really upset and cries a great deal.

"I think I would cry a lot too," I told Tommy and his mum, "if I had to get up every morning at three o'clock and then go and do a full days work at nine o clock!"

Sleep deprivation. What the heck can you do about it, right? Because you are asleep and before you know it you have woken up and as this rule suggests – and anyone with insomnia knows – the harder you try to get to sleep, the more awake you become.

On his first visit I chatted with Tommy about kid things. His XBOX and Game Cube and how exciting they are when you're caught up in the game that three, four or even five hours can vanish, just like that!

Then I helped Tommy appreciate the voice inside his head and he looked at me like I was pretty weird. So I suggested that he try not to finish the next song that I was about to sing, which you, the reader, can now try.

It went along the lines of, "Happy birthday to you, happy birthday to you, happy birthday dear..."

Then I said to Tommy, "Did you hear that little voice inside your head filling in the blanks for you?"

When he nodded I went on, "Well, Tommy, that's the part of you that likes playing on XBOX and your Game cube."

Tommy seemed okay with that. Next I asked Tommy, "Have you had a dream where you can fly?"

Tommy said that he hadn't. I asked, "You're joking, right? You know the dream I mean, right Tommy? Where you can fly about the world and do anything?"

When Tommy still shook his head I said, "You need to have a word with that voice of yours then, Tommy, because the human mind is better than any XBOX!"

Next I had Tommy conduct a little experiment that proved my point. "With your eyes closed, "I instructed Tommy," have your mind design a game that's really fun to play. Now, imagine having a full eight hours at night, playing that game and not having to stop all night!"

Tommy seemed excited by the idea, and promised he would. His mum reported next day that he slept until 7:30 in the morning. It was the first time he'd been able to sleep through the night in months. It was also the first time he'd gone off to school without crying!

How did I manage to pull this off?

- I told Tommy's mum not to acknowledge that she knew me at all!
- Then I talked about the mind and how much better it is than a game.
- 8 hours uninterrupted gaming.
- Then I left.
- Tommy's mum was instructed to ask Tommy where did he know me from, and be shocked at the fact that this strange man (me) had come in and talked to Tommy and then just left. Mum was a brilliant actress. ☺
- **Tommy is now confused, first step before enlightenment.**
- **Bedtime comes and he enters an uninterrupted 8-hour game.**

This last rule proves that the harder your conscious mind tries to do something, the harder the unconscious mind will make achieving that goal. Therefore, we must "trick" the unconscious mind into believing that **change is good for us**.

Fortunately, that's exactly what the rest of this book is going to help you do...

༄

Exercise

1. Consider something that you have been trying to do.
2. Consider doing it.
3. Consider looking back six months after you have achieved doing it.
4. Focus on the feedback that you get between step 1, 2 and 3.
5. Write down what the differences are. Do you have a different voice inside your mind for each step? Do you have movies running inside your mind or are they still images? Are the images in colour or black and white? Do you make yourself small or large?
6. Adjust the sounds and images until you stop "trying" and start "doing."

༄

Chapter 3

Just Because You Say "I Am," Doesn't Mean You Are
"The words "I am" are potent words; be careful what you hitch them to. The thing you're claiming has a way of reaching back and claiming you"

A.L. Kitselman

Who are you?
What defines you?
How do others define you?
More importantly, **how do you describe you?**
Don't answer those questions yet. First, I'm going to try a little fill-in-the-blank exercise with you to start this chapter.
So, now, when I start the sentence, "I Am _____..." how do you fill in the blank? What do you say to complete the second half of that sentence? Here are some popular answers that I've heard clients respond with over the years:

- "I am <u>a father</u>..."
- "I am <u>a mother</u>..."
- "I am <u>a husband</u>..."
- "I am <u>a wife</u>..."
- "I am <u>a daughter</u>..."

- "I am <u>a son</u>..."
- "I am <u>a smoker</u>..."
- "I am <u>an alcoholic</u>..."
- "I am <u>a vegetarian</u>..."
- "I am <u>an employee</u>..."
- "I am <u>a boss</u>..."
- "I am <u>a waitress</u>..."
- "I am <u>an athlete</u>..."
- **Etc.**

There are many ways to describe ourselves and these several are but few of the thousands, the hundreds of thousands, the millions of ways you could choose to describe yourself. But you are unique, and I want you to feel involved in this chapter.

So, below, please answer this question with your own "I Am _____..." sentence:

"I Am _____..."

"I Am _____..."

"I Am _____..."

"I Am _____..."

"I Am _____..."

"I Am _____..."

"I Am _____..."

"I Am _____..."

Now, here's why this is important: When we say, "I am **this**..." or "I am **that**..." we aren't just describing ourselves; **we may actually be limiting ourselves**. When we say "I am **this**..." or "I am **that**..." we give our world structure; we place ourselves in a box. Many of us crave structure, and some of us may even appreciate the "protective" nature of a box.

The problem with putting ourselves in a box is that the longer we stay in there, the longer we say "I am **this**..." or "I am **that**..." and nothing more, the harder and harder it is to see the things that we are excluding that we might be or could be and one day fly beyond the confines.

Boxes are safe, but they don't exactly offer a full range of movement.

Lives are meant to be lived to the fullest, enjoyed and cherished. When we begin labeling ourselves as one thing or another, we tend to cut off the possibilities that exist outside of our known environment.

Our identity starts to become defined much sooner than most of us realise. In many ways that is a good thing, it's vital that we know where we live, who our mums and dads are and which school we go to. We need beliefs and values to enable us to navigate our way through the world. They are the very things that allow us to develop as individuals.

From the messages that are received early on in your life you begin to make decisions about what is right and wrong, what is achievable, and what you consider to be out of your reach. It is this early decision making process that interests me, because this is the area that your Saboteur will be resolutely and unflinchingly policing. Those decisions will, in turn, become your rules, your beliefs, and values. Come what may, your Saboteur will make sure things are kept exactly as they have always been, safe, secure, and unchanging even when you are all grown up and your circumstances have changed. Your Saboteur will be steadfast and unswerving!

Now, that is a fantastic resource to have, just so long as the rules that are being enforced are helping and supporting you, for example, 'I am intelligent and can learn new things easily,' I enjoy meeting new people and make good friends easily. These are perfect rules for your Saboteur to impose, after all, you don't want to have to wander through life, consciously needing to remind yourself every moment that you like meeting new people or you find it easy to learn.

Difficulties arise when your Saboteur is hanging on to a rule that is no longer appropriate. 'Don't talk to strangers' is a great instruction when you are tiny and just beginning to explore the world, but it won't serve you well when you want to make new friends, go out on a date, or find yourself a job.

In order to maintain the wall, that your original decision making created, your Saboteur locks each brick shaped belief in place with a cement, mixed with fear. Some people never manage to break through or climb over their imaginary walls, as the fear of the unknown that lies beyond that boundary wall seams so real. Many of my clients prefer to buy a *Break Through* day with me, committing to a coaching program for a whole day and working with their Saboteur to update those rules and liberate themselves, exciting stuff!

Peter had hit his boundary wall, time and time again throughout his career and now he had set up his own company, but for some reason, this "super star" business man was unable to make any progress or generate an income. His get up and go, had got up and gone! He contacted me for a break through session; he was desperate to move beyond this damaging behaviour.

I'll put his career path to date into a sketch for you, imagine a Toblerone and you've got it. Peter would be employed by a company and within the first year he would prove to be such a shining star that promotions would come his way, his salary would increase, there would be a new company car, he and his family would take another step up the property ladder, and everything would look rosy in the garden. But then disaster would strike. For some unknown reason, Peter would find himself sabotaging his career, so much so that his employers would let him go and he would find himself looking for another job. Then, the whole process would start again. Now, you can see why, when he described that series of peaks and troughs to me, I found myself thinking of Toblerone!

I could go into the details of the ups and downs, but let's just concentrate on the fact that Peter's problem had hounded him for years and the reason he had set up his own company was so that he couldn't be sacked by himself, now could he?

Peter was now in a stand off with his unconscious mind because he knew that he was capable of earning zillions of pounds, but he couldn't make the first step.

"Who would you say are your role models?" I asked.

"I don't have any" he replied unaffectedly.

"What about your father?" I offered.

"No, I am nothing like him!" he retorted sharply.

If you read the last statement again, and this time, take out the "nothing" you will see what I was looking at. A man who was like his father, but was in conscious denial.

I grabbed a pen and began to create a graph of Peter's Toblerone career using his income levels to create the peaks and troughs. I figured that there might be something within his earning bracket that caused him to self-destruct!

Low and behold, every time he fell into the £80k plus bracket, within a year he would damage his career and tumble all the way back down to the bottom and have to start over in another company.

I concentrated on his 'I am' statement, 'I am nothing like him.' (His father)

"What did your father do for a living?" I asked casually.

"I've told you!" he barked, "This has got nothing to do with my father!"

"I know, I know, but humor me," I said, smiling back at him.

"He was a dentist" he retorted.

"His salary?" I questioned.

"This is ridiculous," he growled.

"Treat me like an idiot...." I jested "...and we'll get on fine!"

"About £80k a year..." he said disdainfully "...but what on earth has that got to do with me?"

Then, I went on to coach him through the day, allowing him to see that by holding the belief that he was nothing like his father ("I am nothing like him"), unconsciously, he was putting a huge amount of energy into avoiding everything that, for him, represented his father.

Peter's father was successful in his career and had earned in the region of £80k per annum, Peter measured success by income. So, whenever Peter considered that he was becoming successful in his own career (earning something in the region of £80k), his system would implode. His Saboteur would find a way to uphold the rule that he was the black sheep of the family, a waster, and nothing like his father. To Peter, he was the prodigal son and that's just how his Saboteur was going to keep things.

Now Peter was self-employed, the Saboteur attacked his confidence, preventing him from making the sales calls because they would only result in Peter becoming more successful........ Just like his father!

By the end of that day Peter moved mountains (or is that Toblerones) and after a few follow up sessions he decided to let go of his childhood patterns and spend time with his father. He reported back to me that, in the beginning, "it wasn't easy" as they both cried rivers. That can happen when the barriers come down and there is a shift in your "I am" and your "I am not". It allows you to, not only see yourself differently, but also those around you, your nearest and dearest see you anew. Change one thing and everything changes!

I remember when I first told my dad that I loved him, probably the toughest three words that ever came out of my mouth. It transpired that my grandfather had waited until he was on his deathbed to tell my dad that he loved him. Now my dad was obviously waiting to die before he could say it to me!

Luckily I got in there and began teaching my dad that it was okay for him to say it while he was still alive and full of life. He cried a lot for the first dozen or so times and then he got used to being able to say it, out loud, and as John Overdurf and Julie Siverthorn put it "You never know how far a change can go!"

Lot's of adults continue in the child pattern and wait for their mother or father to say "I Love You" first, after all, they are the mum and dad so it's their responsibility. The truth is that your mum and dad might have been brought up with the same "I am not allowed to mention emotions, or show my feelings rule" as my dad. In which case, let me remind you, there are two sides to a communication, so you know what to do.

Exercise 1

Now you know the power of "I am statements"
Check back over your list of "I am" statements from the beginning of the chapter

- Write down any more that are cropping up for you now.
- Notice if there are any, which might limit you or inhibit your development.
- Check for any patterns.
- Ask a friend to lend a hand; they will spot your Saboteur far more easily than you.

Exercise 2

- Tell your mother and father that you love them; you never know when they won't be here.
- If, like me, you're an orphan, imagine your mother and father to be in front of you, or sitting beside you, and tell them that you love them.
- Tell them that you are sorry for "not forgiving them."
- Allow them to love you back and become whole again.
- "It's never too late for you to have a perfect childhood."

Chapter 4

Beliefs and Values Support Who (You Think) You Are
"Values are like fingerprints. Nobody's are the same, but
you leave 'em all over everything you do"

Elvis Presley

Your beliefs and values define everything about you, right now. So, the sum total of your beliefs and values equals who you are **and** are not today. In other words they support your identity. Luckily, you are a human being, not a marble statue sitting in a museum gathering dust. Life will constantly be bringing you challenges and opportunities that will enable you to change and update your identity. When you grasp the chance to modify your identity, your beliefs and values will change simultaneously. Equally, if you change or modify a belief, then there will be a shift in your identity too.

I'm going to explain how your beliefs and values are intrinsically linked to your identity in the simplest way I know. Consider a table that has four legs and a top, you can see that it looks like a table and when you sit at it with your dinner plate resting on the surface, and it does the job of a table, then you have a table. If you take away one or all of the legs you cease to have a table, likewise, if you only have the four legs, you don't have a table. The table gains its identity by virtue of being whole. Even if you have all of the pieces in your flat pack when it's delivered, it's not a table until all of the parts are assembled as a whole that you can truly see it as a piece of furniture and have it take on it's full identity.

How can a piece of furniture explain beliefs, values and identity? Well, imagine that each component is a strong belief, one leg may represent, 'I am a teacher', another may represent 'I am knowledgeable', the table top may represent 'I am a mother' and the design of that top will be composed of all the beliefs and values that, for you, define 'a mother'.

Every belief we hold gives further definition to our identity, and who we believe we are or are not will dictate our actions and behaviours. Furthermore, it will govern our interactions with others and ultimately give us our aspirations and perceived limitations.

This analogy can be used to look at psychological problems from a different perspective. For example, anorexia or body dysmorphia, the person has all the resources they need to be a fit and healthy individual who eats appropriately and has an accurate body image, but they are unwilling or unable to acknowledge their true identity, hence a struggle begins. It is as if the flat pack came without assembly instructions, all of the components are there, but we just don't know how to put them together correctly. We do our best, but chances are, we will end up with a table that wobbles all over the place.

Did you ever try sitting in a café, having a drink with friends, at a wobbly table? Everybody knows the table is wobbly except the table!

Now, the funny thing is, just as you can look at a table and know if it's safe to sit at or has a leg missing, I can look at you and figure out if you 'have a screw loose' and if you have, that can leave you a little "wobbly" in a certain area of your life.

It always strikes me as unusual that people walk about from day to day never really knowing for sure what they genuinely believe. You wouldn't embark on a long car journey without checking that you have a few essentials like four wheels and a tank of petrol with you, would you? And yet when did you last check what you believe about who you are and what parts of your life may need improving?

I demonstrated this with Christine Fieldhouse, a journalist from a national newspaper. I had met Christine in the past when she had written articles about my work. She had recently written a book about her childhood (Why Do Monsters Come Out At Night?: A Mother's True Story of Two Very Different Childhoods) and she sent me a copy. From reading her story I picked up that she had a few beliefs that could do with an upgrade. I invited her to pick some areas in her life that she would like to improve. These were: work, relationships, self-image, parenting, and money.

Then I asked her to write down as many things as possible that she believed about the areas that she had chosen. Being a fantastic writer, Christine made quite an extensive and detailed list.

I went on to explain to Christine how we all have unconscious beliefs and values that we adhere to, often without knowing, and it is these limiting beliefs that I help a client to upgrade. Your mind will always accept an upgrade, no matter how old you are.

Your limiting beliefs will impact on the quality of your relationship with yourself, your mum, your dad, brothers, sisters, children, co-workers, your house, where you live, the clothes that you wear, the style of shoes that you have on, the types of friends you keep, what you read, if you don't read, the television you watch, radio you listen to, if you smile a lot, or you're a miserable pain in the backside. By adjusting your limiting beliefs your whole world can change, dramatically and quickly! You don't have to wait until next spring to tidy up your mind. You can do it now by writing them all down. At the end of the chapter I will explain how you can work through your list and upgrade those beliefs that are no longer supporting you.

This is how Christine recorded our session. It was used as a main feature in the Daily Express and, as you can imagine, brought a flood of new clients looking to challenge their beliefs and step into a more fitting identity.

"First, Matt asked me to note down all the things my parents taught me about work, so I rack my brain for memories from 40 years ago. My late mum Margaret was my main influence and she had very strict rules. She told me to always do the very best I could; to work as hard as I could, and if I say I'm going do something, to do it, no matter what.

For every belief, we went through a process of writing down the rule and then saying it out loud to bring it into the present and my conscious mind. As I did, I could hear my mum's Yorkshire accent clearly and relived how I felt as a child when I heard those words. Sometimes I felt a determination to do my best and a desire to rise to the challenge, but on other occasions I was overwhelmed at what I had to achieve.

Images appeared in my mind to show how I'd stored these rules in my mind over the years. I pictured a woman flogging a child to make her work hard and an old-fashioned schoolma'm speaking sternly, dressed in black and white. Neither happened to me – my mum was a wonderfully kind woman – but the associations of strictness were vivid.

Once my internal rules were unlocked and my feelings out in the open, Matt started "re-programming" me. Together we altered each belief to bring it up to date and in keeping with the person I am now, not the six-year-old I was. As soon as I read out a new rule, I knew instinctively if it was for me. An old belief such as "always do the best you can" became "I can only do the best I can when I can and that's OK".

Looking at friendships, I revealed how my mum insisted I should never tell friends any personal secrets. Working with

Matt, I turned this into "I can tell my true friends what I want, when I want."

When we looked at my attitude to intelligence, the beliefs of my late father Harry came flooding back to me. According to him, I was clever, but I would always need to work hard. I had no common sense and men wouldn't think I was very bright.

All of these statements evoked memories of sadness, desperation, and a fear of intelligent men. As we worked through them, I realised why I'm happier dealing with women and how I'm much more confident when I'm doing talks about my writing to women-only groups.

Meanwhile, my attitude to being a mother threw up some very old-fashioned legacies, including a belief that women who have children don't have much money. My mum told me this when I was a child – it was probably true in the Sixties when few mothers worked – and I'd held onto this belief and applied it when I became a mum. After playing around with the statement we rewrote it to become: "I have a child and I can make money when I want," which made me feel much more in control.

After leaving the session I felt in transit between the old and the new me. I figured I might believe the new rules for a day or so, and then I'd probably slip back to the old ones. Matt didn't agree: "Take a computer that's been updated from Vista to Windows 7. If it's upgraded, it remains upgraded. The mind is like that too," he said.

Since then I've stood up for myself more, probably because I no longer see myself as a little girl trying to do her very best to please everyone.

By changing just a few core beliefs, I've finally moved from the Sixties to the 21st century. Now I'm working on the next generation by drip-feeding Jack with my new, modern set of rules. Sometimes I slip in a sneaky one to ensure I'm looked after in later years. Well, sons should treat their elderly mothers to luxurious holidays shouldn't they?"

So, there you have Christine's story, now what about yours?

Your Beliefs and Values Will Support Your "I Am..." Statement

The problem that living with a limiting belief creates is that your "I Am..." statements will limit your potential for growth in whatever area of your life it has manifested in. When your parents or guardians gave you rules to live by, some of them were only meant for the playground and to keep you safe whilst you were growing up. "Don't talk to strangers" and "Don't wander away from the house" were great rules when you were aged 4 or 5, but now you are 42 years old and have never gone out into the world because it's scary! Your life is being sabotaged by a redundant rule that you've forgotten about and haven't yet upgraded. Well now you can.

I heard Jamie Oliver's dad installing a beautiful belief/family rule when he and Jamie were talking about marriage, his dad said "The Oliver's are like swans, they marry for life" what a wonderful family rule to have. That will no doubt create a whole set of beliefs and values inside Jamie's mind.

For many, our beliefs and values build up a wall so high our "I Am..." statements become a veritable prison. Remember Iris, from our Rule # **6 of the Saboteur Within:** *Emotional Pains Can Create Physical Change?*

She experienced pain in her knees that was so intense she could barely walk up the stairs. And yet she did, despite the pain, even when she had to balance a tray on her knees so that she could care for her sick, ailing husband.

Iris had an identity; she had a strong "I Am..." statement. It said, "I Am... a wife." That conviction was so strong, reinforced by equally strong values and beliefs, (honor and obey aren't part of the marriage ceremony as often nowadays, but when Iris was young they certainly were) regardless of how she felt personally, or how much she wanted to change or pursue her own interests of reading and relaxing. Her "I Am..." identity forced her to deny her own needs; honor and obey her husband, until she couldn't take it any longer.

What happened then? Her emotional imbalance created physical pain. The only way her conscious mind could combat *The Saboteur Within*, or her unconscious mind, was to literally shut her body down with pain so intense she couldn't walk up the stairs anymore.

She didn't feel any pain when she was relaxing with her Catherine Cookson books, and yet the minute the thumping from her husband's cane sounded on the bedroom floor above her head, the pain flared up with intensity and immediacy.

ᐇᕐᕕ

Parting Words About Who You Are... And Who You Are Meant to Be

"Knowing others is wisdom, knowing yourself is enlightenment."

Lao Tzu

The thing is; it didn't have to get to that point. If Iris had been able to step out of her "I Am" box for a minute, if she'd been able to see her situation objectively and with clarity rather than as a prisoner of her own misguided values and beliefs, she could have realised that being a wife did not necessarily mean being a dutiful servant.

But such is the unconscious mind; it is so eager to have order, routine and safety that it clouds our judgment and makes change seem impossible. It took a full-scale regression and months of therapy to get Iris to see that she hadn't just created an "I Am..." box for herself; she'd created a prison!

Only by breaking free, one brick at a time, could Iris gain relief from the physical pain created in response to her rigid values and beliefs.

You have to ask yourself, how much pain you're willing to suffer before you realise the box you've built for yourself can no longer contain the person you want to be. Indeed, some people would rather die than change. Why? Simple: because changing would upset the precious "status quo" of everyone else and that wouldn't do at all, would it?

∾

Exercise: Your Circle of Life

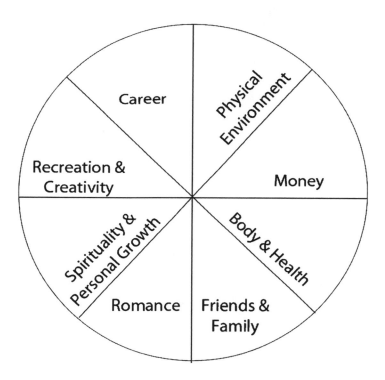

- Take a look at the circle of life and draw a line across each segment at a point that you feel represents your current situation in that particular area, work on a score between 0 and 10 for each area. Now look at the areas where your score is low and the wheel looks like it's not running smoothly and write down what you believe about those areas.
- Once you have written them down, notice if you have any patterns that emerge. Remember to invite a friend in to help you, as someone outside of you will see more than your Saboteur will allow *you* to see.
- Do any of those beliefs limit you, at all? Work with your friend to upgrade your belief.

Example:
"Don't talk to strangers," A brilliant rule for a child.

Upgraded to "It's okay to talk to strangers, when I choose" or "Strangers are friends that I haven't met, yet."

Notice that the upgrade allows you more control, more choice and opens up your world to infinite possibilities.

∽

Chapter 5

FEAR Can Only Come from Experience
"Curiosity will conquer fear even more than bravery will"

James Stephens

I'm going to try a little experiment to start Chapter 5. I'm going to mention two little words and I want you to say the first word that comes to your mind. Are you ready? You don't have to write anything down; no one's going to make you do anything you don't want to do. I just want you to say the words aloud or in your head, okay?

Okay, here goes: **public speaking**!

Are you still with me? Or have you run screaming from the building? (I wouldn't blame you if you didn't come back for a week!) In my line of work, I do a lot of public speaking. The first thing most people say to me as I walk off stage is, "I don't know how you do that every day. There is no way I could get up there and talk to all those strangers, not even for a second!"

Was "fear," "afraid," "scared," "petrified"... or some derivative of all four the first thing to pop into your mind? That's because you can only be scared by something you know **a little bit about**.

Think about it: if you'd never experienced a little bit of fear over being called on in class, made fun of after a wrong answer, dying on stage in the school play, choking during a presentation or giving the wrong answer on an oral exam, you wouldn't know enough about public speaking to be afraid of it!

Fear comes with experience. The more negative experiences we have in life, the more afraid of recreating them we become. The unconscious mind knows this. Remember, it wants to protect you. And what's the best way to protect someone? Fear, there's nothing like being terrified to keep you from doing something.

If you're putting your hand too close to the flames, your unconscious mind will send out fear signals to keep you from burning your hand. Why? Because you've already learned your lesson the first time you burned your hand as a child. It's the physical pain that causes our unconscious to take emergency action and put new rules and boundaries in place to stop that situation happening again. Your Saboteur has sent an emergency memo marked URGENT & CONFIDENTIAL giving him or her information that a new threat has been identified. Instructing that action must be taken to ensure that we don't encounter that same danger or anything that looks similar to it ever again... another brick in the wall!

But in addition to these protective and deep physical fears we have – don't touch that fire, don't play in traffic, don't step too close to the ledge – we have equally real, yet not as equally logical grown up fears that are based in emotional threats.

The fear of losing our job, perhaps. The fear of not being attractive enough, of looking foolish if we dress a certain way, of not sticking our necks out too far for fear of retribution – or failure. The fear of... public speaking.

These **learned fears** can protect us, sure, but they can also be self-limiting and cut us off from the life we're intended to live. It's important that we learn more about the fears that plague us.

What's more, it's vital that we identify those fears that are holding us back:

The Two Kinds of Fear: *Natural Fear and Mind Fear*

Take public speaking, for instance. Ask a class full of five-year-olds to get up and speak in front of the class, show and tell, share a story, do a dance, make a funny face, and every hand in the room shoots up. Ask a room full of grown-ups to do the same, and not only do hands stay down, but everyone shrinks into their chairs, afraid of getting up and speaking in public, of having the spotlight on them.

And yet ... what if you're actually a really good public speaker? What if your words are meant to inspire entire rooms full – stadiums full – of people? What if you have lots to say, and plenty of wit, wisdom, and encouragement to share with the world?

What if, instead of being petrified of standing in front of a room full of people you were meant to do that very thing? What if there is a whole other identity waiting for you; one where you master the art of public speaking own it and live a rich, full, valuable, passionate life speaking to people on a daily basis?

If you can't communicate because of a self-created, self-inflicted fear, you will never fulfill your true destiny. You are not only what you are today. Who you are is fine, but... what if you want more? What if you want to be the next Tony Robbins or Robert Kiyosaki, world famous motivational speakers, but can't because you're simply too afraid to get out of your own way?

I believe there is another destiny out there for you, if you want it; an alternate destiny – if only you'll face your fear and realise that while it can certainly protect you, it can also hold you back and make you less than you were meant to be.

No, this isn't a chapter about public speaking; it's a chapter about fear. About the real fear that is created for us and the equally *real* fear we create for ourselves, often on a daily basis.

Not all fear is created equal. In fact, there are two kinds of fear:

The First Kind of Fear: *Natural Fear*

If there were a hungry lion loose on your street, fear would protect you from walking out the door and trying to pet it while dangling a raw piece of steak in front of its nose.

If there was an area in your city where gangs involved in knife and gun crime spent their time on the street corners, fear would protect you from walking anywhere near there, alone at night – or even during the day. If there were a speeding car coming your way, fear would protect you by making you move swiftly and get out of its path!

That's our first type of fear: **natural fear**. Natural fear is otherwise known as "healthy" fear. Can fear be healthy? Absolutely, you'd be a fool not to be afraid of anything at all, walking into the path of an oncoming car, strolling down a dark alley in a bad neighborhood in the middle of the night or climbing into the gorilla cage at the local zoo! We **do** need fear; we just need to experience it in a protective and not preventative manner.

Natural fear is the kind we feel all of a sudden; it's that "fight or flight" fear that dumps tons of adrenaline in our system, makes our pulses race, our senses more alert and gives us the good sense – and the energy – to get out of the way of a roving lion, a dangerous criminal, a charging bear or a speeding car.

Natural fear is healthy because it physically protects us from harm. But what if our natural fears become unnatural? What happens when we "almost" get in an accident and, from that day forward, never drive again? What happens if we used to love camping and then see a show about bear attacks in the woods and never go camping again?

Remember Barbara, from **Rule # 7 of the Saboteur Within:** *The More You Do "It," The Easier "It" Gets?* To refresh your memory, Barbara couldn't swim. She could listen to the radio and drive a car at the same time, do her job, multi-task many things at once, but she had never learned to swim and the longer she stayed out of the water, the bigger an "emotional boogeyman" swimming became for her.

I was able to use a few psychological techniques to get her not only into the water, but to swim. Remember, I learned that Barbara's reluctance to swim was based on fear; she'd been "terrified" as a young child and the negative emotion had never left her.

Only when she began to associate swimming and its many complex processes with driving and it's equally complex processes, could she get over her "mental fear" and embrace what I call "the swimmer within." Today, of course, Barbara is an accomplished and fluent swimmer who regrets all those years spent sitting by the pool, suffering for her fear; a prisoner to it.

But what if Barbara had never faced her fear? What if Barbara had allowed her subconscious mind to keep building that wall, to keep reinforcing that "box" she'd put herself in that said, "I am not a swimmer; I am a person who does not swim"? She would have been denied a lifetime of happiness, in and out of the water.

So, what's your "emotional boogeyman"? What irrational, unhealthy and unfounded fear is keeping you out of the water, so to speak? Natural fear is healthy fear, until our mind takes over and makes it unhealthy again:

The Second Kind of Fear: *Mind Fear*

I like to say that the first kind of fear is created *for* us; a hungry lion shows up at our campsite, a burglar's at the door, our car starts sliding on a fresh coat of ice. What do we do? We panic, adjust and take action to avoid the very real, very immediate "thing" that's causing us danger; then we act. This "danger" creates fear from the outside in. Unfortunately, the second kind of fear – mind fear – is created *by* us. This creates fear from the inside out!

We've all experienced mind fear, on a daily basis, many of us all day long. Mind fear is fear of failure, fear of success, fear of saying what you want, fear of asking for what you want. Fear of falling in love for the second time (for some reason, the first love isn't there and we don't want to experience the pain that comes with the end of a relationship ever again).

The concern about mind fear is that it's generally not based on a real, literal, or even logical sense of "danger." Let's say you're afraid of falling in love for the second time. You've had your heart broken; maybe you've been betrayed, cheated on, put down, scorned or simply hurt very, very badly.

"Once bitten, twice shy" as they say. The problem is, where is the danger? Fear equates with risk, hazard, peril, and a dozen other synonyms for actual, acute danger. Where is the speeding car, the roaming lion, the hungry bear? Well, in our minds of course, if we're a prisoner to mind fear there IS a very real (to us, anyway) danger in falling in love again.

The pain of that first heartbreak hurt so badly that experiencing it again constitutes a very real threat to our emotional and, in some cases, physical well-being. That's "danger" in my book, right? How about you? Such is the power of the unconscious mind; mental anguish can become so powerful, so insular, so isolating, that the thought of experiencing it again really does cause physical pain.

So don't get it twisted; mind fear is very real fear. We just have to remember that it's based on created danger, not speeding bullets or snapping jaws. And who creates the danger?

The Saboteur Within, of course… doing his/her job and keeping us out of harm's way, guarding us against harm at all costs!

Fear Can Only Come from Experience

Natural fear can come from the shock of burning your hand on the stove or dropping an iron on your little toe, but mind fear typically comes in layers. That's how walls are built, after all; brick by brick, level-by-level, and stone by stone.

It starts at home. Our parents tell us a lot of great stuff about ourselves. They are the ultimate force field against fear, both natural fear and mind fear. They tell us the world is a safe place, a fair place, a just place. They tell us good triumphs over evil, that the wrong will fail the right prevail. They tell us that we can do anything, be anything we set our minds to.

Then, how come we can't all walk on water and achieve anything that our heart desires? The trouble can then be that even though our parents believe in us, sometimes they don't believe in themselves, and as a result, this is the limit that our unconscious mind will set for us. Children imitate what they **see** their parents do and not what they **say**. It is one thing saying you can do anything you like, if they don't demonstrate that by their own actions then that is the response that they will get. Woe betide anyone who should ever try to go beyond it. Suddenly your Saboteur is awake and ready to maintain your already limiting beliefs. That puts a slightly different perspective on "do as I say and not as I do", does it not?

It's not their fault, of course. Like the unconscious mind, they are only trying to protect us. But we quickly learn that some things are beyond our grasp, and that produces in-security; and insecurity leads to self-doubt, and self doubt leads to anxiety, and what is anxiety but an appetiser for... fear?

Over time, in primary school, middle school, high school, university studies, graduation, first job, second job, first wife, second wife, our mind fears escalate. The twittering we heard in the back of the classroom every time we got up for show and tell in nursery gradually blossoms into a fully fledged phobia of public speaking as an adult.

The rejection we learned when we didn't make the football team makes us fearful of any team sport, any organised athletics and, eventually, any kind of exercise at all. We won't go to a gym because we're afraid we might look stupid when we can't figure out the machines. We won't exercise with a friend because what if we're not fast enough, good enough, coordinated enough to keep up?

As a result, the wall gets bigger, the insecure thoughts more frequent and pervasive, until entire areas of our lives – whole banks of opportunities – are closed to us. Such is the danger of mind fear, a shutting off of our world and, as a result, a walling up of ourselves.

It may be safer behind that wall the subconscious has built for us, it may be cosier in that "I Am..." box we've built for ourselves, but outside that box – and those walls – is a world of opportunity waiting to be explored!

Parting Words About Fear

So, what's the biggest problem with fear? Quite simply, **fear is an opportunity killer**. Just think how many opportunities we've missed because of fear. The dates we didn't go on, the trips we avoided, the jobs we didn't apply for, the promotions we missed, the deals we didn't do, or inventions we didn't make, or speeches we didn't give, and songs we didn't sing.

Think back to your biggest regrets in life – be they physical, spiritual, personal, or professional – and chances are they are rooted in fear:

Question: *"Why didn't I hold out for that better price for my house when the first offer came in?"*
Answer: *"Because I was **afraid** I wouldn't get the second."*

Question: *"Why didn't I ever call that girl after she gave me her number in the club that night?"*
Answer: *"Because I was **afraid** I would screw it up somehow."*

Question: *"Why didn't I try out for X Factor when it came to town?"*
Answer: *"Because I was **afraid** I wouldn't be good enough and I'd look a fool."*

Question: *"Why didn't I follow my wife when she stormed out of the house?"*
Answer: *"Because I was **afraid** she didn't think the marriage was worth saving."*

We can't eliminate fear from our lives, but we can learn to tell the difference between a herd of stampeding elephants heading in our direction and opportunity coming our way! Fear creates limits, and ultimately our life is restricted by these limiting self-beliefs.

The bad news is, we're not quite through with fear just yet. In the next chapter, I'll introduce you to what I call the "8 Complimentary Fears" we all face as we go through life. The good news is that knowing them will help us combat them and, ultimately, conquer them.

Chapter 6

The Saboteur Within and Your 8 "Complimentary" Fears
"Our deepest fear is not that we are inadequate.
Our deepest fear is that we are powerful beyond measure.
It is our light, not our darkness that most frightens us.
We ask ourselves,
Who am I to be brilliant, gorgeous, talented, fabulous?
Actually, who are you not to be?
You are a child of God.
Your playing small does not serve the world.
There is nothing enlightened about shrinking
So that other people won't feel insecure around you.
We are all meant to shine, as children do.
We were born to make manifest the glory of God that is within us.
It's not just in some of us; it's in everyone.
And as we let our own light shine,
We unconsciously give other people permission to do the same.
As we are liberated from our own fear, our presence automatically liberates others."
Marianne Williamson

So, why would your Saboteur use your deepest fears against you? Why "sabotage" you at all? Well, it might help if we take a look at your 8 Complimentary Fears and see, specifically, how your unconscious mind uses fears to keep you safe, even if it's not necessarily the best thing for you.

What is a "complimentary" fear? Well, there will always be **natural fear** and **mind fear**; those two "base fears" are non-negotiable. However, modern times have added new and complex layers of fear to our lives, things our prehistoric ancestors didn't have to worry about, like the fear of success or the fear of failure. I call these **complementary fears** because they are "layered" onto our typical mind fears and further hinder us from achieving our true identities.

What's more, *The Saboteur Within* has adapted and folded these fears into new and revolutionary ways to "protect" us while, at the same time, sabotaging our true selves. Beware these 8 complimentary fears, and learn to spot them at first glance so you can overcome them before they overtake you:

∽

Complimentary Fear # 1

The Fear of Success
"Procrastination is the fear of success."

Denis Waitley

What are you prepared to lose?

For you, success means fulfillment, contentment, happiness and pride. But for your unconscious mind, success means that one area it's charged with avoiding at all times and at all costs: **change**!

So, how does The Fear of Success work? Well, in order for your Saboteur to scare the "bejesus" out of you, it will run a series of movies inside your mind showing you many examples of how you will fail to retain your success once you have achieved it.

It's a little like playing "king of the hill." According to the Saboteur Within, the minute you get to the top, someone – maybe even yourself – or something will find a way to knock you back down the hill again. Hence it will flood your mind with images of how you will fail to handle the extra responsibility or additional attention that accompanies your success.

Just as your success motivated you to reach the top, the fear of staying there will become a preoccupation; thanks to the unconscious mind. In order that you may remain "safe" in your carefully constructed world, your Saboteur may convince you so strongly of your inability to handle success that you don't even try to attain your goal in the first place.

Whether it's a new relationship, a job, losing weight, deciding to study and get a better education, or whatever your definition of success might be, thanks to the Fear of Success you might be too afraid to reach for your own dreams.

The inevitable result is that, sadly, the Fear of Success can force you to let these wonderful chances slip through your fingers. If you succumb to the Fear of Success, you will lead an unfulfilled existence, as your Saboteur convinces you that under-achieving is the safe, comfortable and stress free way to be, why put yourself to all of that trouble and worry when you are unlikely to succeed, you won't be able to handle it, or people will think you have got above yourself. These are the type of messages and internal arguments your Saboteur will use against your conscious mind to keep you within the safe and predictable confines of your comfort zone.

When Susan came to my office that day in January, she was desperate to resolve her "sabotaging ways," as she put it. Susan's presenting problem was that she had had several careers during her working life, none of which had made her wealthy, stating that she "always had enough, but never more than enough" and all of her careers had systematically ended when she was offered promotions and much greater financial rewards. In other words, whenever she was given the opportunity to be successful, she would screw it up!

Now, here she was at age fifty-five, divorced, and determined that she could make good. Susan's urgency for the session was because she had been offered a "get rich quick" scam – I mean, scheme (honest!) – she had found it on the internet and the promise that was being made by their sales pitch was that this scheme would deliver abundance and ultimately, "More than enough." The problem was, as she saw it, "her Saboteur was talking her out of this plan she had to become successful."

This seemed the most opportune time for her, as her company was offering her another promotion with all the usual trappings. Susan had been there many times before and she wasn't about to screw up yet another promotion. This time she wanted to break loose of the vicious circle she believed that she was trapped inside, take a risk and reap the rewards promised by the scheme/scam. There was no way that Susan was going to prevent herself from having financial abundance and happiness **this time**!

"Now to fund the scheme," Susan explained. "Rather than accept the promotion that is on offer, I can take voluntary redundancy from my job, and that will give me the cash lump sum I need to buy into the scheme. I don't mind leaving as I am being pressured into taking this promotion and I'm really reluctant to do that, because I will be required to study for an additional qualification, which will mean putting my life on hold for six months while I take the exams that are necessary, and I want everything now!"

I pieced together Susan's life beginning with her family. She was the youngest of six children; she had passed her "11-plus," which allowed her free entry to private education, where in her final year she flunked out of school. I will get deeper into the unconscious patterns another time, but for now let's simply say that Susan was afraid of being successful because she thought that she would be an outsider, to the rest of her family, the odd one out with the spotlight clearly shining on her, and highlighting the fact that she was 'different'.

You see, when Susan flunked out of school, it was because being one of six kids, and suddenly propelled out of her home environment, she never felt that her family was behind her. Yes, when she first got her scholarship it was exciting and everybody talked about it when it was news, but now, four years on, Susan was fast becoming a "cuckoo" in not only her school, but also her family's nest. It seemed that she didn't feel at home in either place.

Her Saboteur mounted a double-pronged attack. In order that Susan could remain within the status quo of her family, where nobody had excelled academically in the past, her personal Saboteur Within filled her mind full of thoughts, like, "Who do you think you are?", "Nobody likes a clever clogs!", "You talk too posh", "You're not one of us anymore!" and on and on, making Susan feel out of place in her own home. Whilst at school the posh, fee-pay-ing students made fun of her less than posh accent and made cruel remarks about the part of town that she lived in. Eventually, Susan cracked under the pressure of feeling like a cuckoo in her family's nest and she quit the school, as success meant that she would remain an outcast.

"So Susan here we are," I finally said to her. "Forty years on, only six months, and one exam to allow you to be suc-cessful and have financial freedom."

Susan nodded uncertainly before I added, "Or, we work on what you've asked me and I encourage you to throw it all away and gamble your hard earned savings **and** your redundancy payment on a scheme that, if it fails, leaves you jobless and broke! It sounds to me like your Saboteur has brought you here to continue an old pattern."

Susan's face was crestfallen; she'd never heard it put in such blunt terms before!

"Let's examine the two scenarios in front of you," I said calmly.

"In the first one you gain financial freedom and status, which will allow you extra cash to put into schemes, yes?"

Susan nodded.

"And the second will have your whole family talking about you and worrying as they have done many times be-fore, hmmm! It sounds like there is a Saboteur at work some-where," I smiled.

Susan took a deep breath and admitted, "The truth is, I've taken that exam three times and failed every time! I don't know what it is! I can do the job standing on my head. All of the other exams to get me to this level I got straight A's but this one... I just go blank when I sit down to take it."

After her confession, Susan sighed heavily.

I told Susan about Jonathon Livingstone Seagull, how even as a seagull he had ambition and how his flock was very uncomfortable with his dreams and aspirations. In or-der to achieve his goals and fulfill his true potential, he had to overcome the worries and concerns that his friends and family raised, not only in an effort to keep him safe from, but also trying to ensure he didn't show them up to be lacking in courage and imagination. *Jonathon Livingston Seagull is a terrific book by Richard Bach. It is packed full of wisdom and will only take you a couple of hours to read.*

Then, in laymen's terms, I explained that the Saboteur was preventing Susan from getting what she wanted because it would mean that she was successful. The status that went with it would change this duckling into a swan and her Saboteur had filled her mind full of thoughts that boiled down to, "You're not worthy!"

Tears welled in Susan's eyes as she stared off into space, running through all of her past examples, where the finishing line was within her grasp and she failed to take the final steps.

Susan was a smart woman and she sat there open mouthed as the realisation of how her Saboteur had been playing her, her whole life long, but not this day. Her lips came together with a resolute pout and a solid determination concretised her as she said, "Today is the day that I turn my life around!"

As we worked through the coming months, with her fear of success long gone, Susan effortlessly passed her exam and was very comfortable with her new company director status.

ᦒ

Complimentary Fear # 2

The Fear of Failure

Thinking

If you think you are beaten, you are;
If you think that you dare not, you don't;
If you'd like to win and you think you can't
It's almost certain that you won't.

If you think you'll lose, you've lost;
For out in the world you'll find
Success begins with a fellow's will -
It's all in the state of mind.

If you think that you are out-classed, you are;
You've got to think high to rise;
You've got to be sure of yourself before
You can ever win a prize.

Life's battles don't always go
To the stronger or faster man;
But sooner or later, the man who wins
Is the man who thinks he can.

Walter D. Wintle

We have all been stung by failure. Be it in a job search, a spurned romance, or a rejection of any sort. Few things hurt like a resounding failure, but unfortunately failure is a part of life; particularly a part of modern life.

To our prehistoric ancestors, of course, failure meant not eating dinner. For us, failure could mean foreclosure, bankruptcy, unemployment, being alone, being overweight… even homelessness. Yet the more we fear failure, the more we stop trying to do things we might fail at in the first place.

This becomes like a Catch-22 of fears as you cling to a rigid timetable and routine, terrified of ever putting a wrong foot on your life's journey lest you might wind up in the poor-house – or with NO house. The Saboteur whispers to you and reminds you of your past failures which, in turn, will prevent you from making decisions as – reminds the Saboteur – "you will probably make bad ones anyway."

The Catch-22 comes from the fact that you fear failure so much, you actually welcome failure. In other words, you are actually failing by virtue of not allowing yourself to fail.

Consider Frank's story. Frank was a high-flying club promoter who lived the high life for nearly a decade. He drove exotic cars, went to the best clubs, brought along his rich, fancy, influential friends and made incredible amounts of money to basically party all night. Frank used to boast that "wine, women and song" were part of his job description!

Then someone told him he wouldn't be clubbing forever, that he should make a few wise investment decisions before he lost his hair. He listened, and invested in several commercial buildings, right before the real estate bubble burst. Frank lost everything, the cars, the high-rise apartment, the trappings, the friends... the lot.

But what Frank lost most was his self-confidence. He became so afraid of failure; he couldn't even continue to do his job. He never again thought he'd make that same kind of money, so he quit even trying. He looked up a former client and secured a job as a bartender, preferring to work at an unambitious job for a steady paycheck rather than ever risk the type of overexposure that had put him at risk in the first place.

The sad thing is, Frank "failed" (more like the economy failed) in a field completely outside of his own. But fear is repeatable; Frank felt if he could fail so badly in real estate, then what was to prevent him from failing in club promoting as well? A failure is a failure; regardless of the line of work he's in... right?

The antidote to this fear is to use logic.

There is no such thing as failure; all you ever get is feedback!

So, if you're walking along the road and you trip, the failure is in not seeing the obstacle that you tripped over, whilst, the feedback is to make sure you look where you are going.

"From the ashes of disaster grow the roses of success"

∾

Complimentary Fear # 3

The Fear of Rejection
"If you love someone, set them free.
If they come back they're yours; if they don't they never
were."

Richard Bach

If you touch a hot stove burner once, chances are you'll never do it again. If you cut your foot on a piece of broken glass in the kitchen, chances are you'll wear shoes until all the broken pieces are found and disposed of.

So what happens when you approach an attractive person to ask for a date... only to get turned down? Will you ever do it again? For many people, unfortunately, the answer is "no."

This fear is a spin off from The Fear of Failure as it, too, is a painful Catch 22. Your Saboteur will convince you that you can never be accepted by anyone, and to even think that you might, will only leave you hurt and humiliated. And so, according to the Saboteur, the best way to live a pain-free life is to never approach anyone and always reject any offers of friendship as you will become fond of them and, no doubt, they will reject you at some point in the future anyway, and that will hurt even more!

If your Saboteur has convinced you of this, then you will appear very aloof to others and people will be able to feel the temperature drop around you. Brrrrr! You will appear as a very cold person, and yet the warmth of a serious, committed relationship is the very thing that you crave. If you fear committing to others, you won't just be hurting them but yourself as well.

Much like the Fear of Failure, the Fear of Rejection is a self-fulfilling prophecy. You fail because you don't try, and you don't get rejected because you don't try. Yet inherent in never being rejected is never creating relationships where you might get rejected, hence living a lonely, isolated and solitary life.

And who wants that? Kim didn't; she hated getting rejected – hated it! So instead of getting rejected, she became aloof, distant and unapproachable. She made sure to always do the rejecting before anybody else could possibly, potentially reject her. Over time, she found the easiest way to reject others before they rejected her was to simply avoid people altogether.

Even at work, with people she saw every day, she would appear cold, distant, and unapproachable. Those who dared approach her would get a helping of sarcasm, followed by irony, topped off with condescension; they quickly learned never to do that again! The sad thing is, Kim wanted to be loved; and she had a lot of love to give.

Underneath that brittle exterior was a person so vulnerable she simply couldn't stand to be rejected anymore; hence her "reject first, hurt less" attitude. One mourns for the life she could have had; the fulfilling relationships she missed out on because of her fear of rejection.

❦

Complimentary Fear # 4

The Fear of Not Being Liked
"We are afraid to care too much, for fear that the other person does not care at all"

Eleanor Roosevelt

The Fear of Not Being Liked is yet another Catch-22 syndrome. You go out of your way to be liked, only to find yourself unconsciously alienating those you want to like you the most!

The Fear of Not Being Liked sets in when the Saboteur convinces you that you must **keep everybody happy** so that they will all "like" you. The result is that you will imagine what will make others happy and act as if what you imagined is real for the other person. All the while, that person has no knowledge of what you have decided they want or need, so your actions can result in some unexpected and unwanted reactions.

You will apologise for everything in advance so as to maintain – or gain – approval. In the end, this will often turn you into a needy and most unlikable person, giving you the opposite result of what you wanted to achieve.

James was suffering with this problem when he came to me for coaching. His wife had basically forced him into having some development sessions with me because their relationship was going through a rocky patch.

James was a smart, well-mannered, and well-spoken gentleman. I could best describe him as a Labrador. Just in case you don't know what I mean, it's very simple; a Labrador is a breed of dog that is loyal, faithful, and does what it's told!

James was working ridiculously long hours for his employers and he was just unable to say no to them. We worked on the fact that when he said yes to them, in effect, he said no to his wife and children. James knew this was the case and it made him feel bad, but he kept on doing it. His employer certainly wasn't going to call a halt to this procedure; after all, they were getting extra work done and not having to pay anything extra. James clearly understood the logic of this and was well aware how upset his wife was about it, but still the Saboteur continued to have him say yes to his company.

This is very a common problem for many people, so here is a common answer. I coach people through this scenario regularly.

When you are asked to do something that you don't want to do but saying "No" is too scary for you, say "No, not at the moment but if things change I'll come back to you" or any sentence that you can come up with that contains that same theme.

By using this approach, you are practicing saying "no" without the need for feeling bad. It's really neat and you can start using it straight away!

Remember, you can please:

- **Some of the people, all of the time**
- **All of the people, some of the time**

But you can't please:

- **All of the people; all of the time.**

Instead, give yourself – and others – a break by just being yourself. Don't run down your self-worth by being a 100% people pleaser, 100% of the time.

All you can do is your best, and trust that others will love you for it. To further illustrate this Thomas A Harris, did an excellent job in his book "I'm okay you're okay"

Four life positions

The phrase I'm OK, You're OK is one of four "life positions" that each of us may take. The four positions are:

1. I'm Not OK, You're OK
2. I'm Not OK, You're Not OK
3. I'm OK, You're Not OK
4. I'm OK, You're OK

The statements are self explanatory, principally in any relationship we are looking for "I'm OK, You're OK" a lot of relationships limp along in step 1, 2 or 3, leading to all sorts of human conditions. The 4th position allows both people within the relationship to grow, develop, nurture, and encourage one another.

∽

Complimentary Fear # 5

The Fear of Loss
"Nothing can ever be truly lost, merely transformed"

The Saboteur does a really good job with this particular fear. If this is one of the layers that your Saboteur has created, you will be convinced that everything in the universe is measured out and, what's more, everything is in extremely short supply. Therefore, you will have the feeling that there "Isn't enough, love, happiness, compassion, money, well-being, laughter, employment, education, etc, etc, etc, and finish the sentence with.... in the world."

Your Saboteur will have you so convinced that you won't buy expensive things, as it would be too painful if you were to lose them. Heaven forbid that you should ever even consider falling in love, because your loved one would die eventually and leave you alone, so you sabotage your relationships right at the beginning before they amount to any value. This is yet another paradox as you lose the chance to love and to be loved by fearing the loss.

One extreme symptom of the fear of loss is hoarding. Brian was once a happy family man who lost his job thanks to an injury and quickly snowballed into losing everything, his family, his home, his car, and his football card collection – all of it.

While he eventually got back on his feet and found a new job – and a little house that he could afford – Brian never forgot the pain of that loss.

He spent every extra penny he had – and many he didn't – on things. It didn't matter what; he never wanted to run out again. Soap, detergent, canned peaches, three of his favorite style of shirt, and ANYTHING on sale!

It soon got so bad he could barely walk through his house, so he rented a storage space – and quickly filled *that* with things. Unfortunately his hoarding got so out of control that when a neighbour called round with a parcel for him and saw how he was living, they called in the city council. They made many attempts to persuade him to clear the rubbish from his house, or at least allow them in to do so. He would not co-operate, so they ended up fining him £10 a day for every day his home was uninhabitable.

He eventually lost his home – and his possessions – and had to live in his storage shed, which naturally had to be cleared out to make room for him. In the end, he lost everything – again, but only because of his deep Fear of Loss!

~

Complimentary Fear # 6

The Fear of Helplessness
"Fears are educated into us, and can, if we wish, be educated out"

Karl Augustus Menninger

People who experience The Fear of Helplessness know that the Saboteur Within exists, so they become obsessive about control in their life, thinking that this will give them ultimate power. They can't ever relax, not even for a moment, because if they do their world will come crashing down around them and they won't be able to put the pieces back together again.

If this is the fear that keeps you locked in, everything is measured within your world; you have your days planned out for months in advance. Friday is fish night; sex is on Sunday morning between 8 and 9 am. All things are measured to within an inch of their lives and let there be no spontaneity because that comes from unpredictability and, ultimately, leads to chaos!

Paradoxically, the Saboteur is actually fuelling the fear, so the individual tries to close their life down into systems and measurements, believing all the while that this will calm the fear. But guess what? This only magnifies it!

Remember "Barbara" from **Rule # 7 of the Saboteur Within:** *The More You Do It, The Easier "It" Gets?* Barbara had been terrified when she was thrown in the water as a young child and remembered the experience as making her feel very pained, very exposed, very… **helpless**. As a result, she wished at all costs to avoid appearing helpless – ever again.

Here she was, at a beautiful resort, enjoying her family **by** the pool, but never enjoying the actual experience of being in the pool with her children for fear of being helpless. By avoiding one emotion, she was shutting off her entire world; and shutting out those she loved by not fully involving herself with them and all of their activities.

The people who experience this very damaging fear, eventually end up helpless, as their struggle to keep life, chaos and infinite possibilities out of their world can be totally exhausting. This can lead to a sense of futility about their lives, and ultimately becoming a fear that prevents them from ever relinquishing control. If you were to stand up for a moment and place a small coin between your butt cheeks, pull your cheeks tightly together and hold on to the coin, you will now have a sense of how it is for this person and they are doing it twenty-four hours a day, seven days a week!!!

Complimentary Fear # 7

The Fear of Separation
"Be true to your heart and the person in the mirror,
Then you can never be alone"

M.Hudson

You're probably thinking to yourself, "Matt, I'm an adult. This fear is surely for a child, isn't it?" The answer, sadly, is "No." Why? Because the Saboteur will convince you that your world will end if you let that special someone out of your sight. You will define your life by being a part of them. Without them, you will rationalise, you cannot be a whole person.

Cinderella's father is a good example of this. When his first wife died he felt lost and worthless. Suddenly, enter the new wife and bam! He feels whole again and is blinded to the pain and anguish that his daughter has to live through as a result of her wicked stepmother and ugly sisters.

Despite the pain to others, your Saboteur will convince you that you need this person in order for you to exist. Therefore, you will reject your family and friends in order to survive. How? By letting this single person dominate your entire existence, all due to the Fear of Separation.

In reality your fear is yet another Catch-22 as the tighter you "squeeze" the other person, the greater the probability is that you will choke the life out of your relationship and separation will ensue (and all because of your claustrophobic actions). In the Charles Dickens Novel *Oliver*, Nancy had this fear with her partner Bill Sykes and the result is there for all to see.

The Saboteur may go so far as to close down your health and well-being causing you to become weak and frail. The upside is that you get to place your loved ones in shackles, so that they can't wander off!

Susan fell in love with Ron at first site. He was everything that she needed in a man: tall, dark, and handsome. Oh! I forgot to mention he was also... **married with children**!!! This didn't stop Susan from hanging around Ron at work all day. Eventually, one day the short "hellos" developed into coffees and lunch. Ron was a flirt with a twinkle in his eye and very soon broke his wedding vows. Susan made it her business to tell Ron's wife, who promptly showed him the door. Ron moved in with Susan and all was well in that house... but not for long.

After a few months of living together, the Saboteur eventually begins to whisper to Susan, "He will leave you on your own." To safeguard herself, Susan falls pregnant and all is well, but whilst pregnant Susan lost her curvy shape and that brought about a deeper fear...did I mention Ron's twinkling eyes? Susan was worried that he would be off with the next young woman, the same way she had caught him. What to do? What to do?

Susan thought that if she could keep Ron at home, then no woman could ever steal him away. The only problem was she couldn't very well say out loud, "You're not allowed out," because that might make him run. No, that wouldn't do at all. The plan needed to be subtle. So subtle in fact, that Susan could never have come up with it without the help from the Saboteur Within.

Her Saboteur's plan was foolproof; to begin slowly, gently, piece by piece, delivering excruciating pain. Just a little twinge at first, needing to take a few painkillers and lie down here and there, but very soon, Susan would be so unwell that Ron would be unable to wander off out for a drink with his friends. Meanwhile the Saboteur continued to whisper more loudly and more frequently, "He'll leave you! He'll abandon you!" Susan's pains grew worse and worse and Ron's leash got tighter and tighter. Finally, unable to stray, his eyes became lifeless as little by little the sparkle was extinguished.

At the time of our meeting, Susan had four children to Ron and was on a maximum dose of painkillers. After many, many hospital visits and talks with physicians, no cause could be found for her pain, nor could they prescribe medication to bring her relief. By now Ron, too, was on medication, anti-depressants, in an attempt to try and bring back the sparkle to his now dead eyes.

Susan presented as a pain client and as we explored her story through a few sessions, we worked on the secret guilt that Susan had about stealing another woman's husband; the torment of life's boomerang coming back to bite her. As we alleviated these issues bit by bit, Susan was able to let go of her fear of separation. As the fear ebbed away, the pain diminished and the Saboteur was re-deployed to support Susan in getting slimmer, fitter, and healthier.

Two years on Susan and Ron have a whole new dynamic within their relationship and Susan lights up the twinkle in Ron's eyes without the need of a pharmacist.

The fear of separation doesn't just take root in romantic relationships; Brenda was an example of how this fear can take root in all sorts of areas of our lives. At the age of 47, she was living with her five sons, their partners, and even her mother had moved in when her father had passed away.

Recently, Brenda's husband, Trevor, left after 27 years of devoted marriage, saying he was "worn out." Suddenly, Brenda sat like a spider in the centre of a huge web, woven from emotions, anxiety and fear. Nobody moved without Brenda knowing and nobody did anything to upset Mum.

The fear that ran through Brenda rubbed off on her sons who, although grown men, were still treated like little boys, causing friction and tension with their female partners who, quite rightly, wanted to be in a relationship with a grown man and not a child still tied to his mother's apron strings. Brenda was consistently clipping the wings of her children by telling them that she only wanted what was best for them and when she felt really comfortable and confident with them flying the nest, then – **<u>and only then</u>** – could they leave home.

Secretly, the Saboteur Within Brenda was sabotaging the future of the whole family in order to maintain the status quo. Wanting to remain forever comfortable, with her fear of separation forming, her emotional "spider web" that, just like the real thing, tangled her precious treasures tighter if ever they tried to make a bid for freedom.

෧๏

Complimentary Fear # 8

The Fear of Vulnerability
"To fear vulnerability is to fear the consequence of truth"

M. Hudson

Have you ever heard the saying, "His bark is worse than his bite?" Chances are the originator of that saying had **Fear # 8:** *The Fear of Vulnerability*. In other words, those who bark the loudest are often the most insecure, the most scared and the most vulnerable.

Your Saboteur uses The Fear of Vulnerability against you to prevent you from being rejected. Most people who endure the Fear of Vulnerability have very low self-worth and to mask this with behaviours that can look just like the opposite is true, your Saboteur will ensure that you appear "tough" and "arrogant" to the outside world.

Stuart was a very good example of this particular type of complimentary fear. He was sixty-five years old when we first met and he was a very, very angry man. Stuart had suffered a heart attack and a quadruple by-pass at age forty, and as he walked into my office that first day I was immediately able to sense the tension, which, I commented, "Came into the room with him."

It took several sparring sessions with Stuart before we finally managed to get to the heart of his **fear of vulnerability**. His presenting problem was an undiagnosed choking feeling that he said was "with him constantly." I felt that this tough guy needed to see that I too was a tough guy who had found a better way of coping with life before we could have a chance of doing any real work. You see as a coach/therapist/trainer you have to be prepared to flex and take on many roles, much like an actor, and if I was to help Stuart in getting to his outcome, it would be an easier path for him to follow if he could clearly see that I had walked that route first.

It transpired that Stuart had never had a good relationship with his father, who, according to Stuart, had never shown affection to him. Little Stuart learnt very quickly from his relationship with his father that, "You are on your own in this life and no one will look after you but yourself!" This mindset was to set the tone for a lifetime of fighting; arguing, arrogance, isolation, remorselessness, and anger – one of the seven mortal sins – that continued to block Stuart's spiritual development.

The Saboteur worked relentlessly inside, causing Stuart to attack anything that even remotely looked like friendship. At school he became a bully and created lots of problems for anyone who tried to get close to him.

All the while he was pushing people away, Stuart secretly wanted affection; he longed to be held and loved by his own father. The fire would rage inside him and be fueled relentlessly by the Saboteur for many years to come. Not one tear would he shed for any one, not even upon the death of his father. "Good riddance!" cried the Saboteur as the feelings of that day only sought to pour petrol onto the bonfire of ire, which was Stuart's "daily bread."

I had to be careful here; discretion and subtlety needed to be my closest allies. To have told Stuart in our very first meeting that his fear of vulnerability had contributed to his heart attack would have alerted his Saboteur and sent him running out the door.

So, step-by-step and inch-by-inch, I offered rational, irrefutable logic, which built the bridge between us. For example, I would talk about the vast research that has been done to correlate anger and heart attacks, strokes and poor respiratory health. For example, Harvard

Medical School, in one study of 1,305 men, found that angry men were three times more likely to develop heart disease than calm ones. Stuart was able to see that there was sound science behind the information I was giving him and, as our trust began to forge more strongly, he became more and more comfortable with himself and the world around him.

His wife reported back that she had at last, after forty years, got to be with the man that she always knew he could be and, some two years later, Stuart has been able to engage with his own spiritual awareness, appreciating the strength and courage behind making himself at ease with vulnerability.

Up to this point in time The Saboteur had worked uncompromisingly to support Stuart's fear of vulnerability. Imagine, if you will, every friendship offered to you scorned and love thrown aside like a used tissue. Luckily, we were able to meet and I was able to cajole Stuart along this leg of his own personal journey.

Anger, denial and bullying may keep your secret safe for so long, and your Saboteur will maintain this rigid stance for you. All at the expense of being flexible and opening yourself up to love.

Ultimately you are loveable, although the rumors within your mind would have you believe otherwise. And others will rarely know how lovable you are behind that angry, hostile exterior, because you spend your entire life pushing them away, and all to avoid any situation or relationship that could bring you anywhere close to vulnerability.

Parting Words About Your 8 Complimentary Fears

Beware these complimentary fears when you begin seeing the signs. These are very, very common fears that most of my clients present with at least one of them; no doubt you were nodding your head here and there as you read through them.

Maybe you can relate to one or two of the above fears, maybe more – maybe all. It's not how many complimentary fears you can rack up, but how many you can identify and, therefore, conquer.

∽

Exercise

1. Think about something that you are afraid of.
2. Form a statement of your fear and write it down.
3. "I am afraid of .... because............
4. Ask your friend to help you in digging for your many meanings.
5. Sit back, close your eyes and allow yourself to imagine being somewhere that is both fun and relaxing.
6. Whilst you are in this wonderful state of mind, have your friend repeat the meanings back to you, quietly.
7. See your fears way off at a distance as though you are watching an old black and white movie.
8. Continue this for approximately twenty minutes.
9. The key is in how relaxed you can become and how much fun you can allow yourself to imagine!!!

Chapter 7

A Limited Self-Belief
"Where belief is painful we are slow to believe"

Ovid

"I can't...."
"I shouldn't..."
"I mustn't..."
"I wouldn't..."
"I won't..."
"I didn't..."
"I don't..."

Why is it that we always revert back to what we *can't* do versus what we *can*? What we *didn't* do versus what we *did*? It's because the Saboteur Within has created a series of beliefs about ourselves that produces a kind of "default" setting that feels comfortable, familiar and above all - safe!

Even if it closes the door on possibilities.

Even if it keeps us down.

Even if we're not entirely happy; at least we're... safe.

In many ways, self-beliefs are necessary for structure and order in our lives. After all, every day can't be full of chaos and disorder, can it? Even a daredevil needs to know where his parachute is or what mountain he's climbing next!

The problem is that most of us eventually become limited by these self-beliefs. Which is, of course, exactly what your Saboteur Within wants. After all, if you believe yourself to be **only** a shop assistant, a waitress, a manager or a teacher, there is less fear of you, say, opening your own business, running a marathon, asking for a promotion, or switching careers in your mid-50s. Why? Because this "**only**" compounds the limits of your world and your Saboteur will stand guard at your prison gates. To save you risking the dangers that lie in the unknown beyond the safety of those carefully built walls.

Self-Beliefs Limit Us

The fact is; self-beliefs are often limiting. That's because life is easier that way. Better to be lonely, disappointed, broke, and fat – if that's your "comfort" zone – than nervous, anxious, fearful, and even hopeful about a possible life change.

At least, according to the Saboteur Within.

I know what you're thinking: "Why doesn't my conscious mind start and kick the subconscious mind's butt?"

Good question; I hope that you are beginning to formulate your own answer?

The Three Keys to Transformation

When I was twenty-six years old I developed chest pains when walking uphill and even climbing stairs. I had always been fit and, at the time, I was young, energetic, and other than those recent chest pains, felt totally invincible, so this was a bit of a conundrum for me. I just couldn't understand it. I'd never smoked or done anything that would harm my body, so what on earth could it be?

My doctor diagnosed me with angina and prescribed the appropriate medication for my presenting condition. Whilst giving the doctor my medical history, I became consciously aware that my eldest brother died at age twenty nine of a heart attack and several of my uncles had passed away before the age of thirty five, all with heart attacks or heart related illness.

My doctor explained that I would go through a series of tests that would allow them to check my heart thoroughly. But I wasn't out of the woods just yet. In fact, as I waited for my appointment at the hospital, things got progressively worse and I wondered if they would ever get "better." In the months that followed I got weaker and weaker as the "illness" took hold.

Eventually the day came when the specialist checked out my heart via a CT scan. Great news at last: the scan showed that my heart and the arteries around it were clear of any blockages, or indeed any other problems or disease. The consultant was happy, although not quite as happy as I was! Over the next couple of months my breathing became normal again, what was left of my medication was returned to the doctor's surgery to be disposed of, and the chest pains vanished.

So, what had happened? Why had I suddenly grown short of breath at the ripe old age of 26 when there was no physical reason for it to happen? And, once informed of my "diagnosis," why had things taken a sudden turn for the worse until I got the test results back?

Clearly, my Saboteur had earmarked me to follow in the steps of my big brother, my role model, and all the other men folk in my family. After all, I had been hearing from various relatives all my life how the males in our family die at a very early age and this will have been a topic of conversation at countless family meals, holidays, and get-togethers. Living with that constant reinforcement, who was I to imagine that I might be allowed to break the family "curse"?

Thinking back, it was quite an eerie prospect to think that I too could have fallen foul to the Saboteur Within me. This time I was lucky enough to understand and acknowledge that the family's beliefs didn't need to be my own. Today,

I have three sons who require their dad to be around for many, many years and that's the role that I have set my Saboteur to fully support me in.

I was very lucky to have my wife Sonya around during my brush with the Saboteur, because she was on the outside giving me a direct feedback loop to all that I was doing, saying, and being. For her insights, observations, and simply holding up a mirror to enable me to fully see, I am eternally grateful.

According to Joseph Yeager, there are three things that have to take place in order to enjoy an effective transformation:

1. You have to **want to change**
2. You have to **know how to change**
3. You have to have **the time to change**

Fortunately, my angina diagnosis was a blessing in disguise as I was able to breakthrough the "dead by thirty five belief" which, now it was out in the open, seemed ridiculous; I didn't smoke, hardly drank, and was otherwise fit and healthy, so other than this belief there was nothing stopping me from living a long and happy life.

Wherever you are in life, right now, at this very moment, seize these three keys to transformation and never, ever let go!

∽

Confusion: *The First Step to Eliminating Your Limiting Self-Beliefs*

"Confusion is the final step before enlightenment"

∽

When my client Mr. Watson, a school headmaster, asked me if I could "work some magic" on a six-year-old student who had a terrible stammer, I smiled and said, "Of course."

I had been working with young children for a few years in private practice by then, and Mr. Watson had retained my services, on an ad hoc basis, to support any children in his school with behavioural problems. There was a lot of red tape as usual, but Mr. Watson always looked out for the child's interests above anything else, and would do what he needed to do to enable me to work with his pupil.

The day arrived and I was invited into Mr. Watson's office. Mr. Watson then left and collected little Jimmy from his class. I'd like you to keep in mind that Jimmy's "Saboteur Within" was utilizing his stammer to capture more attention, mostly from his parents and the world at large. This meant that Jimmy would need a new strategy to help him to move beyond this developmental stage.

While I was alone in the office, I sat in Mr. Watson's chair so that when the two of them came back, they would have to sit on the other side of the desk. Mr. Watson looked very puzzled as he walked in and sat down on the wrong side of the powerful desk. He said nothing other than to introduce Jimmy to "Mr. Hudson."

Jimmy was a freckled-faced, ginger-haired, young boy, with, I was informed, a terrible stammer. "Do you like Bart Simpson?" I asked. Jimmy looked puzzled, so I repeated the question, adding that Bart was "my favorite character." Jimmy smiled and nodded in total bemusement.

I then went on to explain that, while watching an episode a few days earlier, the show began to run "out of sync." Suddenly, Bart's mouth was moving but Homer was speaking. "It's frustrating, isn't it?" I said to a now curious Jimmy.

The young boy stared back at me with a knowing look on his face.

"Then everything has to STOP, Jimmy!" I said with some energy. "And when everything is STOPPED, Jimmy, then everything can be realigned so that everybody is speaking with their own voice. Now, isn't that interesting?" Before Jimmy had a chance to respond, I dismissed him with, "You can go back to your classroom now, Jimmy; thank you."

As a bewildered Jimmy left the headmaster's office, an equally bewildered Mr. Watson sat staring at me and wondering what had just gone on.

"Matt," he said, in his Edinburgh twang. "You can't expect me to cough up for that?" I took that to mean he didn't want to pay for my latest "performance." I remember mentioning to him that I was feeling a little like the Pied Piper after ridding Hamlin of its rats; the people of the village that had been plagued by rats were suddenly unwilling to pay now that the problem was gone and the piper had rid them of the rats!

The headmaster raised an eyebrow and looked at me, his face filled with doubt and disbelief; I smiled at Mr. Watson knowingly, enjoying the view from behind his big wooden desk. "Trust me on this one Phil," I said.

"All right!" he said, extending his faith in me, at least for now. Then he chuckled, "Can I at least have my bloody chair back, now?"

The next day Mr. Watson rang me to say that Jimmy's mum and dad were at the school and little Jimmy had woken up **without his stammer**.

"How the bloody hell did you do it?" asked a now fully-trusting, amazed although still confused Mr. Watson.

"Elementary, my dear Watson," I replied wryly.

What I did, dear readers, was to utilize all of the information that I have given you in this book. Let me explain in detail; Jimmy had a limiting belief about being a "stammerer", in other words, one of his "I am' statements would have been, "I am a stammerer", and in order to save him from his Saboteur Within, I would have to use his many other beliefs to erode and eradicate this one. To see better how I accomplished this goal, let's have a look at the session from Jimmy's side of the desk.

Question: When does a child go to the headmaster's office?

Answer: When you've been really **good** – or when you've been really **bad**.

The headmaster is usually behind his large, imposing desk. So, if there is someone else sitting in the head's chair, and Mr. Watson doesn't tell him to move, not only that, he just sits quietly on the 'wrong' side of the desk alongside Jimmy, then that person must have more power than the Head.

This 'powerful' person likes the Simpsons, just like me.

This person gets frustrated, just like me.

If I haven't been bad, then this person must have something... good... for me?

All of the above are positive beliefs. Now, by not allowing Jimmy to talk, I prevented him from identifying himself **to me** as a "Stammerer." Then, by dismissing him without explanation, I maintained his confusion while still feeling good about himself. Finally, I had seeded a strategy for Jimmy to let go of his stammer. This way Jimmy would be puzzling over our conversation all day long and as he sailed into sleep that night, everything would STOP for Jimmy. The next day Jimmy had **stopped** and then started again – *without* his stammer.

Yes, there is a method hidden within my madness and more often than not, as Milton Erickson the psychiatrist, psychotherapist, and hypnotherapist that revolutionised Western psychotherapy, would put it: "any explanation is a therapeutic mistake."

What Erickson meant by this statement, is that the client already has all the answers they need to resolve their issue; as therapists, we just have to find a way to propel our clients above and beyond their current definition of themselves, outside the boundary of their self-limiting beliefs and into chaos and confusion. It is in that confusion that they are able to tap into the infinite possibilities that are there for all of us if we do but dare to take that step and transcend the threshold of our self-imposed 'safe house'.

Always be aware, your Saboteur will use fear to keep you 'safe', but it's all an illusion, **F**alse **E**vidence **A**ppearing **R**eal; chaos is nothing to be feared.

Remember: "Confusion is the step before enlightenment." So don't be afraid to be confused; it's the first step to eliminating your limiting self-beliefs.

෧

If

If you can keep your head when all about you
Are losing theirs and blaming it on you;
If you can trust yourself when all men doubt you,
But make allowance for their doubting too;
If you can wait and not be tired by waiting,
Or, being lied about, don't deal in lies,
Or, being hated, don't give way to hating,
And yet don't look too good, nor talk too wise;

If you can dream - and not make dreams your master;
If you can think - and not make thoughts your aim;
If you can meet with triumph and disaster
And treat those two impostors just the same;
If you can bear to hear the truth you've spoken
Twisted by knaves to make a trap for fools,
Or watch the things you gave your life to broken,
And stoop and build 'em up with wornout tools;

If you can make one heap of all your winnings
And risk it on one turn of pitch-and-toss,
And lose, and start again at your beginnings
And never breathe a word about your loss;
If you can force your heart and nerve and sinew

To serve your turn long after they are gone,
And so hold on when there is nothing in you
Except the Will which says to them: Hold on;

If you can talk with crowds and keep your virtue,
Or walk with kings - nor lose the common touch;
If neither foes nor loving friends can hurt you;
If all men count with you, but none too much;
If you can fill the unforgiving minute
With sixty seconds' worth of distance run -
Yours is the Earth and everything that's in it,
And - which is more - you'll be a Man, my son!

Rudyard Kipling

Knuckling Down: Getting to the Root of Self-Limiting Beliefs

When my wife, Sonya, was diagnosed with rheumatoid arthritis in her early thirties, she was busy running her own hairdressing salon, raising four boys (including me!), and had less than no time to be ill.

Sonya's hands were giving her massive pain, so much so that she had to take time out of her salon, cancel appointments, and attempt to rest her hands for so many hours a day. To a committed workaholic like Sonya, she didn't know which was worse: the pain or the time off from her loyal customers!

We were fortunate enough to be able to see a consultant rather quickly; who suggested an operation would be the best way forward. The plan he suggested would be to remove Sonya's knuckles and replace them with plastic ones.

"Wow," I thought. "What a wonderful idea? NOT!!!!"

This was a time when a second opinion was definitely needed, my own! So, knowing what I knew about the Saboteur Within, Sonya and I decided to use hypnosis to engage **directly with the Saboteur** and create a whole new set of outcomes for Sonya and her hands.

After our first session the swelling in Sonya's hands had gone down considerably and the pain eased. The second session brought about more flexibility and the third session, some ten years ago, saw the end to Sonya's pain, outcome; no operation, no drugs and no side effects.

So what happened? Where had the pain come from and why did it go away? Sonya's spirit was encouraging her to embark on her own path at the salon, but her own personal "I am" message was trapping her inside her beliefs about being a mother, a wife, a provider, a worker and on and on. The conflict this created manifested in pain in her hands making it impossible for her to continue juggling these different identities.

We worked on upgrading Sonya's beliefs around her identity and in so doing, uncovered a need to explore a more spiritual and therapeutic focus to her work. She has long since left behind her scissors and hairdryers and become an exceptional hypnotherapist specialising in past life regression.

She would be the first to tell you that letting go of her expectations of herself in respect of her identity as mother, wife, provider, and even hairstylist, allowed her to move beyond the conflict she was experiencing and create a fulfilling and rewarding career.

Many people continue to struggle on through this conflict and use alcohol, doughnuts, or prescription drugs to help them, but that gives rise to even greater illness, pain, and depression.

Take for example, Bi Polar disorder or manic depression as we used to know it. You see a famous person on television who has more money than they could ever spend, famous friends, and a super star lifestyle, yet they are suffering with Bi Polar disorder. How can this be?

Well let's look at the chemicals that their brain creates for them. They are enjoying their starring role, their hit record, their moment in the headlines, and all of that produces excitement and in turn their brain creates an intoxicating cocktail of chemicals that gives them that elated, walking on air, got the world on a string feeling. Then their equivalent of Monday morning comes, the run on Broadway ends, someone else grabs the starring role in the hot summer blockbuster film, and the paparazzi have taken up residence on another doorstep. All of a sudden, their natural chemical rush has reduced to a normal level, big problem! OMG!!! Help me doctor I'm suffering from depression, the next big film role or TV reality show comes along and all of a sudden they are on a high again. Their roller coaster life style creates an addiction for the rush, which comes with this territory.

What they are really suffering from is an attack of the 'normals'! Life has natural ups and downs, the true test of how well adjusted and flexible you are is making lemonade when you're given lemons.

I have worked with celebrities who have been on prescription anti-depressants for over twenty years, when what they really need is to be told that it's normal for them to feel low and then to build a set of strategies for feeling good about yourself without the dependency on an external stimulus.

Imagine that your mind has a setting from zero to ten about how you feel about yourself. Now ask yourself on an average day, zero being low and ten being high, what number do you give yourself? At what point on that scale do you start your day?

Most people start their day on a two or a three, so it doesn't take much to be feeling really bad about yourself and the world around you. What if you were to start your day on a seven. That gives you room to fall in love, get a pay rise, drop a dress size, or win the lottery, whilst also leaving you the capacity to deal with a flat tyre, getting caught in the rain, or learning that the boiler won't make it through another winter.

People who feel good about themselves can roll with the ups and downs that we all encounter in life without having to turn to an outside substance to get them through the day.

In the many client examples that I have drawn from, you can see quite clearly how you could end up with bi-polar, both mental and physical pain, insomnia, ME, etc. In fact if you were to consider the nature of your Dis-ease, it will come down to un-easiness within yourself and no amount of outside influence will bring you back into balance, unless you allow yourself permission to let go and grow.

∾

Chapter 8

Generalisation, Deletion and Distortion
"Your eyes will only affirm or deny what your mind believes"

Noted thinker and linguist Noam Chomsky posed a revolutionary theory in the late 1950s that suggested all sentences in the human language have both a deep structure and a simple structure.

By adapting Chomsky's theories, and studying great therapists Milton Erickson, Fritz Perls, and Virginia Satir, researchers Richard Bandler and John Grinder created NLP (Neuro Linguistic Programming). A fundamental part of NLP is something known as the Meta-Model, which is a pragmatic communications model, largely a method of questioning used to specify information in a speaker's language.

Central to the Meta-Model is the theory that we never communicate an event as it actually happened. Instead, we tend to modify it through three very basic filters:

- **Generalisation:** *Making General Conclusions About Any Given Event*
- **Deletion:** *Omitting Details or Facts from a Significant Event*

- **Distortion:** *Modifying How You Describe a Significant Event*

∽

Generalisation: *Making General Conclusions About Any Given Event*

"Men are more apt to be mistaken in their generalisation than in their particular observations"

Niccolo Machiavelli

Generalisation is a valuable tool that allows us to take one-time learning and generalise it. Take opening doors as an example, from being tiny babies, almost from the moment we are born, we watch people come and go through something that we fairly quickly come to identify as a door. And, before long, we are able to try them out for ourselves. Unconsciously we are saying, "Well, I know how to open the doors in my house, and all doors must be similar, so in that case, I must be able to open any door in any building."

Generalisation is valuable because it helps us learn, adapt, and move on. Without generalisation, we would have to relearn how to open a door, tie our shoes, or drive a car every single day.

Unfortunately, generalisation as applied to our mental, emotional, and spiritual lives has certain dangers. For instance, when we generalise about people – or certain types of people – we can fall into traps that look and sound dangerously like racism or nationalism. Assuming that the acts of one person means that "they all" act that way can lead to limiting beliefs about an entire race, group, or nationality of people.

It can also lead to limiting self-beliefs about ourselves. Remember, generalisation is a simple tool for making our lives easier; tying our shoes, opening doors, shifting gears in a car. When we try to extrapolate this tool to our emotional life, it may make things simpler, but it hardly makes them healthy.

Emotionally speaking, for instance, generalisation makes us "always" go for the bad boy, or date the aggressive female, or avoid women/men who are "just like" our exes. It encourages us to label certain "types" as good for us – or bad. But by now we should all know that this is a limiting self-belief. How many women or men who look like our exes could actually be "good" for us, if only we opened ourselves up to the opportunity to get to know them?

"Maggie" is a great example of **generalisation**.

Did you ever meet someone that you sensed just plain didn't like you? They just gave you that blank look or stared straight through you, like you weren't even there! Well, that's just what Maggie did to me.

I was giving a talk on Unconscious Communication, standing up there in front of my audience; it was easy for me to see everyone's face. I was able to clearly see Maggie, sat safely in the centre row, unreachable, untouchable, and safe, or so she thought! It was a great event and the group all had a great learning experience looking at the different levels of communication that go on during a conversation.

When we broke for coffee, midway through the lecture, I walked up to Maggie and said, "I'm not him!"

She looked at me in a confused way and said "Sorry?" in a tone that said, "I don't believe I heard you correctly."

"The guy who hurt you," I added. "I'm not him!"

Maggie was a little bewildered as she asked, "How do you know about... *him*?"

I explained that I could feel the energy disconnection between us and since we had never met before, and as I held her in unconditional, positive regard, it made sense that she was running a generalisation pattern on me.

Ergo, she had had a bad experience with a guy and, as a result, all men were now bastards!!

I went on to explain that, "Unless you do something to break this generalisation pattern, you will continue to play the 'ice woman' when all the while you want to be loved. But you're scared that you will get burned again, so you don't allow any man to make a connection with you."

Tears welled in Maggie's eyes as she stammered, "I d-d-didn't mean to f-freeze you out, Matt. I didn't even realise that I was doing it!"

Salt water is always a good sign of an emotional shift and sure enough the frost melted from around Maggie's aura and we finally connected. "Not all men are bastards," I chuckled. Maggie smiled a warm smile and her generalisation was now at an end.

Good thing, too, because if that behaviour had been allowed to continue, then her Saboteur would continue to maintain a wall of ice between her and anything looking remotely like her ex, i.e. most men on the planet!

I think you'd agree that this was not a healthy position for moving forward through life. Such is the danger of generalising too much – or too often.

In another case, let's say your dream job was always to work for a greeting card company. You grew up making cards for your friends and family, writing them in your head, maybe even illustrating them, and worked hard to gain a qualification in creative writing, only to wind up with a junior position at your very first greeting card company right out of college.

Only… well… the experience was dreadful. Your boss was an egomaniac, the company was badly run, there was a strict chain of command where only senior people did anything creative, and you found yourself a glorified office junior in a very unhealthy, very dysfunctional company.

You leave after only one year, completely disheartened, disappointed and disillusioned. Generalisation would have you believe, as would your unconscious mind (aka Saboteur Within), that ALL greetings card companies are run this same way. You decide that you should give up on your dream and do something else instead, because obviously the world of greetings cards is a disaster area and not as you had imagined.

But... but... they're not all run the same way. You don't hate greeting card companies, just *that* greeting card company! Maybe this was the WORST greeting card company in the world and you just happened to work there first. There are 101 other wonderfully run, welcoming, nurturing, creative, and efficient greeting card companies just waiting to find someone as passionate, educated, and experienced as you.

If you give in to generalisation, and instruct your Saboteur to declare greetings card companies a danger zone then you are missing out on your dream.

∞

Deletion: *Omitting Details or Facts from a Significant Event*
Yesterday upon the stair

I met a man who wasn't there

He wasn't there again today

Oh, how I wish he'd go away

When I came home last night at three

The man was waiting there for me

But when I looked around the hall

I couldn't see him there at all!

Go away, go away, don't you come back any more!

Go away, go away, and please don't slam the door

Last night I saw upon the stair

A little man who wasn't there

He wasn't there again today

Oh, how I wish he'd go away

"*Antigonish*"

William Hughes Mearns

The other morning while shaving I was shocked – shocked, I tell you! – To discover several grey hairs. I thought to myself, "Where did those come from?" After all, they certainly weren't there the day before.

I counted them; there were eight. Eight grey hairs. I promptly brought them to the attention of my wife Sonya, who just as promptly stated, "But Matt, you've been grey for years…"

But… but… how could this be? The fact is, I'd clearly been "deleting" the fact that I had grey hair from every image I saw of myself, almost as if my Saboteur was operating a special edition of Photoshop in my head. Why would I ever do such a thing? The answer is simple: it all goes back to my own personal "I AM" statement.

Who am I? Clearly, "I am a young man…" Have been for years, I tell you! And young men don't have grey hair, so naturally my Saboteur Within will help me unconsciously overlook, deny and delete actual information that others can plainly see.

So, what's the real danger in deletion? Well, while it's clearly more "pleasant" for me to walk around life, denying and deleting that I have grey hair, the fact is when we allow ourselves to enjoy a distorted "I Am" vision, we are really only living half-a-life.

Youth is, in fact, overrated; at least when you've grown into a wiser, more mature and experienced man. Imagine the limits my self-beliefs have put on myself as I go about my day, acting as a young man, and not putting to good use all of my valuable life experiences, credentials, and hard-earned wisdom.

This was much the same story for Kevin, who, when he booked his sessions with me, had a presenting problem of low self-esteem and a fear of public speaking. Kevin was a sales director for an international company with thirty years experience under his belt, yet, for some "unknown" reason he had recently started to feel that he knew nothing!

We chatted about his career journey and he told me how when he started out, all of the older members of the sales team were "useless", and didn't have what it takes to be a good salesperson!

Kevin had recently celebrated his 50th birthday and there, in that fact, lay the key to unlocking his problem. A few weeks into his fiftieth year Kevin had a big problem something he had never experienced before.

For years he had stood up in front of audiences and spoken with ease and authority about his products. He had even handled hecklers well. Now all of a sudden he was breaking out into a hot sweat at the very thought of talking to a few of his colleagues around the boardroom table.

Kevin had always treated the older sales professionals at his company with contempt and, on the morning after his significant birthday, he was suddenly faced with a 50 year old, "an old man", staring back from the mirror. His Saboteur had worked tirelessly over 30 years to ensure that he was top dog within his field, while also wielding a sense of arrogance and disregard toward any older people, full stop! His "I Am" statement was, "I am young and vibrant and energetic, and tech-savvy, and eager, and motivated, and anyone over the age of 49 is not."

Here, nine months on from that massive life distortion experienced on his own 50th birthday, Kevin was suffering at the hand of his own Saboteur. All of the things he believed about older people not being any good at anything, being clumsy and unable to do the job properly, were now acting against him, the poor "old" guy!

So, just like my grey hair, we would work on all of the positive things about becoming, wiser, more mature, and experienced, the obvious facts about the over 50s that Kevin had spent years deleting. Together we transformed those deletions into supporting beliefs, new instructions for his Saboteur, which would allow him to forge ahead, regardless of his chronological age. Inside of a month Kevin reported back that he was back in the saddle, with even more skills than he could ever have had as a young green horn, fresh on the job.

In both instances, our Saboteur was working to support our "I Am," for better or worse, usually for the worse!

What are your beliefs about age? Write them down below and you may surprise yourself!

Being 40 means....
Being 50 means....
Being 60 means....
Being 70 means....
Being 80 means....
Being 90 means....
Being 100 means....

If you find that you have been a bit harsh with some of your answers, ask a friend to do the exercise with you, and then you both have an external person to give you feedback.

༄

Distortion: *Modifying How You Describe a Significant Event*
"I know that you believe you understand what you think I said, but I'm not sure you realise that what you heard is not what I meant."

Robert McCloskey

We all know people who have a distorted self-image of themselves. Often it's for the better; more often than not, it's for the worse. For instance, Steve is a salesman for a local restaurant supply company who lives, acts, and talks as if he is the next Alan Sugar. He is never NOT selling!

Steve lives large, looks good on paper, and believes every word out of his mouth is a license to print money. But his life is a series of mixed messages. He drives an expensive car and lives in a hovel. Why not the other way around? Well, no one ever sees his home but everyone sees his car; this way he can continue the delusion that he is far, far more successful than he actually is.

In a word, Steve is distorting his entire life.

If Steve goes on a sales call that goes badly, he will verbally distort, repeating it thusly: "The buyer is small-minded and needs a small-minded company; that's not who I represent. He'll be ready for me next time!"

If he goes on a date that ends badly, he will distort some more, explaining, "She was too intimidated to be herself. Watch and she'll call first thing next week!"

Distortion allows Steve to paint every scenario in his favor, whether or not it actually worked out that way. Now meet Sally; Sally uses distortion to downplay every advantage she has – and she has many.

Sally is a hairdresser with a booming business, but can't – or won't – take any credit for it. "It's the location," she'll tell anybody who remarks upon her busy salon.

When someone compliments her latest style she'll say, "Oh, so and so could have done it much better."

If Sally goes on a great date, she'll say, "I'm not sure he liked me very much."

This trend leads us to something very critical in our learning at this stage:

Analysing the Dunning-Kruger Effect

The way our mind is able to distort information is absolutely fascinating and, as such, was worthy of a scientific study performed in 1999 by Justin Kruger and David Dunning, subsequently referred to as the Dunning-Kruger Effect.

Wikipedia says "... Dunning–Kruger effect is a cognitive bias' in which an unskilled person makes poor decisions and reaches flawed conclusions about their own abilities, but their incompetence denies them the metacognitive ability to realise their mistakes. The unskilled therefore suffer from illusory superiority, rating their own ability as above average, much higher than it actually is." [**Source:** http://en.wikipedia.org/wiki/Dunning%E2%80%93Kruger_effect#cite_note-Kruger-0]

We've all seen the Dunning-Kruger Effect in action: the painful, shrill, tone-deaf singers who are flabbergasted and outraged when Simon Cowell and the other judges on Britain's Got Talent, hit the buzzer and give them a reality check. On the other hand, the highly skilled often tend to underrate their abilities, suffering from illusory inferiority. Susan Boyle, the runner up of that same show in 2009, is a perfect example of this: someone who is bemused, confused, and disbelieving when the world gives them the feedback that they are **truly amazing**. It's like, well, the Dunning-Kruger Effect in reverse!

"This leads to the perverse situation in which less competent people rate their own ability higher than more competent people. It also explains why actual competence may weaken self-confidence: because competent individuals falsely assume that others have an equivalent understanding. Thus, the miss-calibration of the incompetent stems from an error about the self, whereas the miss-calibration of the highly competent stems from an error about others." [**Source:** http://en.wikipedia.org/wiki/Dunning%E2%80%93Kruger_effect#cite_note-Kruger-0]

I'm sure we have all experienced being invited to dinner by someone who has convinced you that they are **a fantastic cook**. You arrive, salivating with anticipation at the culinary delights that will be served and then find yourself sitting next to good old Dunning & Kruger trying to hide a grey, glutinous mass under your napkin, and wondering just how quickly you can make your excuses and leave before the chip shop closes!

Both Steve and Sally are under the spell of the Dunning-Kruger Effect as they distort, to opposite ends of the spectrum – but for absolutely the same reason: **to support their individual "I Am" statements**. Steve's statement is known as "illusory superiority." He says, "I am the best sales-man in the world" and all his distortions match this statement.

Likewise, with her "illusory inferiority," Sally must think, "I'm not particularly good at anything, I really don't have much to offer" and, similarly, all her distortions support that "I Am" statement as well.

So, what do your distortions say about you? Keep your eyes open for Dunning & Kruger or the Distortion Filter when you are out and about. I assure you, you will be amazed at how common – and potentially dangerous – it is.

Parting Words About Generalisation, Deletion, and Distortion

The fact is; generalisation, deletion, and distortion are all part of modern life. We have so much input coming at us, we often have to "cut corners" just to survive; generalisa-tion, deletion, and distortion help us get through the day, do our jobs, maintain our relationships and keep our "I Am" statements, intact.

The problem is that all three contribute to *comfort*, not growth. Remember, I am not here to make you feel more comfortable; I'm here to make you feel more alive! Generalisation, deletion and distortion are a fundamental part of our lives but you don't have to blindly follow them and find yourself living only half the life you could have.

Instead, learn to recognise when you're generalising, check for deletion and start to "delete" distortion. Fully en-gage with life and create an entirely new "I Am" statement to support you.

◦◦

Chapter 9

I Am or Not I Am – That is the Question
"We carry within us the wonders we seek without us."

Eric Butterworth

In order for us to learn anything new, we have to be able to let go of the old. That's why people don't change because to change you have to get to the edge of your beliefs and values and find a way to change your "I Am."

The challenge is, changing your "I Am" statement, or trying to, can **appear** to lead you to a very, very scary place:

Let me share with you a very common statement that I hear from so many of my clients: "I am unlovable." It may not fall from their lips in those exact words, but once we have chatted about their presenting problem and dug a little below the surface of some of the "I Ams" they have offered me, it becomes abundantly clear to me that a limiting belief of "I am unlovable" is at the root of the problem. Why do people feel unlovable? It can come about in tens of thousands of ways, more than likely; it is the result of some deletion, distortion, or generalisation way back when they were tiny. That is when most of our beliefs and values, both supporting and limiting, take root. Something happens, real or imagined (deleted, generalised or distorted) and it can cause a great deal of emotional pain. Our highly defensive and ever vigilant Saboteur leaps into action and puts measures in place to prevent us ever experiencing that particular problem ever again. Avoiding action must be taken at all costs.

The problem is not that you suffered a hurt of some sort; the problem is that your Saboteur cares about you so much that he/she takes no chances with their precious charge whatsoever. The Saboteur doesn't work with specifics, so anything that even vaguely resembles that hurtful situation must be attacked, avoided, eradicated, or exterminated. Just imagine an angry dalek on guard to protect you everywhere you go, and you might begin to see how your interactions with other people could create the impression that you aren't all that lovable. It doesn't take long before 'I am unlovable' literally becomes one of your belief statements.

As hurtful as it is to hear, as shocking as it might be for your family and friends to imagine you thinking in this way, if your beliefs and values from four years old or even younger tell you that you're unlovable, well, that's what you'll believe and, as a result, that is how you will behave. Remember, your Saboteur Within will do everything in its power to support that belief. You may not have started out unlovable but, so strong is your belief; you'll certainly act it.

How? The how can manifest itself in an infinite number of ways, by pushing others away, acting the fool, by being ungrateful, selfish, boorish, or even excessively sugary sweet and self deprecating not to mention a million other ways. By whatever means your Saboteur feels is the most foolproof and safe, you will achieve the self-fulfilling prophecy that you are unlovable, that way, your Saboteur feels, nobody will ever get close enough to hurt you again.

Unless you get out of your box and start thinking differently, that is!

Mandy was in her late 40s when we first met. She was a very smart looking woman who was extremely self-sufficient. Her presenting problem, not that she would have ever called it a "problem," was that she had had long relationships in her past but they always seemed to be with men who were emotionally dysfunctional.

So, she wanted me to help her find out why she was attracted to this type of character trait. Did you ever wonder about the type of people you gravitate towards or who make a beeline for you?

Mandy gave me various descriptions of her exes, who fell into two prime categories:

1. They were either **unavailable men**, who one day would suddenly "remember" they were married and end the relationship or...
2. **Available men** who she would become bored with at some point and, ultimately, reject of her own accord.

"Would you describe yourself as lovable?" I enquired nonchalantly of Mandy during one of her visits.

"I can see where you might think that" she replied somewhat coyly, "what with me still being single and all."

Now I was puzzled, because even though I was asking a straight-forward question. Mandy's answer didn't make sense.

"In what way does your present relationship status mean that you're lovable?" I inquired with the utmost curiosity.

"Well, it's exactly that!" she replied, suddenly inspired. "Look at me; I'm still single and none of my relationships have lasted," she replied matter-of-factly.

"Mandy, you've confused me! How does that make you lovable?" I asked.

"Lovable?" she asked. "Lovable?? I thought you said "*Un*lovable'!" Mandy now looked bemused, as the words drifted around inside of her. She was actually unconsciously deleting the word "lovable" and replacing it with "unlovable," which would go a long way to supporting Mandy's relationship hang ups.

"I've never thought of myself as lovable before" she confessed, avoiding my eyes.

"So are you?" I persisted.

"Am I what?" she replied, as if no question had been put before her.

"Are you lovable?" I asked for the umpteenth time.

Mandy squirmed in her chair looking very uncomfortable. "What do you mean?" she deflected once again.

"I mean, are all tiny babies lovable?" I quipped

"Yes" she responded without hesitation.

"And you were a baby?"

Mandy nodded.

"So you were lovable, yes?" I queried

"I suppose so.," she said sheepishly.

"Then who told you that you are anything else but lovable, then, now?"

Even as a therapist or coach, when I come across the negative "I Am" statement it still takes a great deal of to-ing and froing and some serious digging before the client can even begin to recognise the existence of the "Not I Am" statement: This is something that is totally outside their conscious thoughts, there is no way they could be aware of these patterns and explain them to me. The Saboteur will have been taking care of this so long and so effectively the behaviours that support the belief will happen automatically, just like breathing.

∽

The "Not I Am" Statement

"How can I know who I am when all I know is who I am not?"

Matt Hudson

The "Not I Am" statement is any statement that is the opposite of the "I Am" statement – or everything that you currently believe is not you. The unconscious mind is working tirelessly to maintain your status quo, your sense of self, and your "I Am" statement. Therefore, anything that can cause conflict with your core self-belief will be sabotaged out of existence via your deletion, distortion, and generalisation filters.

Sometimes, by simply bringing your "Not I Am" into your awareness your Saboteur may simply transform all of your negative associations into positive ones; don'ts into dos, cant's into cans and over a relatively short period of time, you can emerge as a **different you**.

This works because deep inside of you there resides a higher consciousness that is ready, able, willing, and waiting for you to remember that you are always more than whatever, or, whoever you think you are. You are always more than your current "I Am" and if you define your world as a fixed, solid mass, then you are also defining and solidifying your problems within that world.

Therefore, if a therapist, coach or a friend is ever to actually help you, they have the challenge of having you realize that by accepting your "Not I Am" into your reality, it will in fact magically transform your reality.

Mandy could fully appreciate being unlovable and she had countless examples of how this was exactly the case. Her "checkered" past relationships had been with men who were also "unlovable," so neither Mandy nor her exes were able to fully open up to each other. After all, that could mean that one of them – or even both of them – were actually lovable, AAAAAGH!!!!!

Imagine how terrifying that would be to the status quo? Far better to remain unlovable with all of the familiar emotions that brings up. The concept of being "Lovable" lay strictly outside of Mandy's awareness, within her "Not I Am" or her infinite possibilities. This meant that we would work to redefine all of her counter examples, until she could say, "I am lovable" – and actually mean it.

A week later whilst brushing her teeth, Mandy called to say that she had found herself smiling back at herself in the mirror and thinking, "I am lovable." Now, with her Saboteur busy enforcing the new supporting belief, she would be able to begin her life again and attract what she wanted and **not what she didn't**.

My own personal journey has had its fair share of chaos and challenges, but of course it has been those periods of chaos and confusion that have been my greatest teacher. Giving me insights into life have enabled me to help many thousands of people find the key to their own potential. Lao Tzu said, "The journey of a thousand miles begins with one step". So, let me share with you some of my own steps, which have brought me to be the me I am right now. Hopefully, a story from my journey may help you to take another step along your path....

༄

Who Am I and Who Can I Be?

"When I let go of what I am, I become what I might be"

Lao Tzu

When I was young, I would spend many days climbing trees when I should have been at school. When you have severe hearing difficulties like I did and nobody knows, not even you, then sitting 60-feet up at the top of a tree, out of harm's way seemed to be a very good idea indeed.

Back then, schoolteachers had their favourite weapons of torture, ones they were very keen to exercise on a daily basis. Especially with a young, seven year old lad, who spent a lot of his time daydreaming, imagining how to live forever, and staring outside, beyond the pain. Back then, I could never really understand why I was punished for not listening, but sure enough another lashing would come my way, just the same.

It was during those formative years when I couldn't hear that I learned all there was to know about non-verbal communication. I could tell by the twitch of the maths teacher's eyebrow that the blackboard rubber was going to be launched into the air and would be heading my way...again!

Home was a rented council home where my mum, Edith Lavinia Hudson, nee Malpas and Dad, Charles Nelson Hudson, both worked hard to bring up their family "properly."

Mum was an eternal child; she had the ability to get on with anyone, always having a kind word. She was to be my inspiration for Getting Rid Of Fat Forever (GROFF) , my highly successful weight loss programme that uses humour to explore the unconscious reasons people over eat. Rather than looking at faddy diets and extreme exercise regimes, which never worked for my mum, she was always overweight and always on a diet. The family doctor would sit behind his desk, bellowing at her to lose weight and take more exercise. Mum would leave his surgery in tears after failing time after time to lose the pounds on his prescribed diet. From mum, I would learn both humility... and fun.

The doctor didn't know it, but his verbally abusive lectures taught me a lot about hypocrisy. He would sit there, engulfed in a cloud of cigar smoke, a huge, obese, walrus of a man, with rosy cheeks, which he carefully maintained by sipping, intermittently, from a whisky glass – all while instructing my mum how to lose weight!

Dad started his day at five every morning, come rain or shine. It would be years before I would appreciate him fully. He allowed me to grow and be who I wanted to be. "I have to work to keep you all," he would say. I wrongly thought of myself as a burden to him, but in all of my life, when my pals were being beaten at school and then again at home, my Dad never raised a hand to me.

I asked him about this a few years before he passed and he said, "My dad hit me and I swore I would never hit you." Dad was stoic in his work, yet when he came home he would come upstairs to my bedroom and tickle me with his bristly-whiskered face. From dad I learned integrity, honesty, and truth.

I had two brothers: Geordie, the eldest, and Nelson, the middle son.

Geordie was my role model. A natural born entrepreneur, he travelled far and wide and lived his life to the maximum. Dying of a heart attack at the age of twenty-nine, when I was fourteen, would leave a massive gap in my life and set an unconscious belief within my young teenage mind - one of a short life expectancy. Whenever I hear Elton John's "Daniel," I think of Geordie and, even now, as I write, a tear comes to my eye as I recall our childhood together.

Nelson was a gentle spirit who had special needs. I was four years younger than my delicate brother and so would spend my time defending him and fighting with the other kids in the street when they made fun of him. The area I lived in came to be known locally as "Dodge City", so, as you can imagine, there was no shortage of conflict and confrontation. Through Nelson I would learn about judgment, injustice, inequality, and non-diversity.

Margaret, my sister, was the eldest of the four siblings. She left home upon the birth of her youngest brother, and would eventually be all there was to connect me to the family as Nelson would die at age forty-five of a heart attack. Margaret and her husband, Bob Richardson, were inseparable; they had one child, Jason, and would hold the torch for me to follow. Thankfully, they were out there shining a light, as there would be some very, very dark times ahead.

When I met and married Sonya, she had a son, young Alan. Very soon, she was pregnant with our own son, Karl.

I worked hard to create a decent income, but being fresh from the air force, I was more than a little naive and far too trusting of everyone, this would cost me dearly. One dark night, the darkest that I had ever encountered, the Saboteur would move in for the kill.

&

Suicide: *A Permanent Answer to a Temporary Problem*

&

Sonya gave birth to Karl; a fit, healthy, perfect baby boy. Why would I even consider being worthy of such a gift? You see at the time I desperately wanted to provide for my family as my father had done for me and every attempt I made turned to dust. Another business fraudster parted me from the last of my money and the pressures were mounting.

"How can I be a dad?" I asked myself, among other questions.

"Why is everything going wrong?"

"Why can't I do anything right?"

The "Why" questions, with their accusatory tone, would send my mind into a tailspin. "My wife and family needed someone who can look after them," I muttered to myself. "I am useless! I am worthless!" The voices continued inside my mind for days and then weeks.

Until one Sunday evening in October. That was when the answer, the only answer, the easiest and fastest answer imploded inside my mind: DEATH! Yep, that would fix everything; the Saboteur confirmed it by finally stilling the voices inside my head. I realise that this might sound quite sinister, but actually if you follow the Saboteurs rulebook, I needed to have a quiet mind, a sense of purpose, something I could achieve and quickly. In this instance it would appear that the Saboteur was bringing an end to my very existence, when what he was actually doing was supporting my desperate search for a purpose and direction that would solve my problems. Suicide would deliver everything that I needed and it could happen instantly!

I emptied the contents of my pockets onto the bedside table, taking only my bus fare, one way, to town. Saying nothing to my darling wife, the mother of my firstborn child, I left my keys and closed the door, for what I believed would be the last time, I stepped into the foreboding night.

The journey to my demise was calm and measured. "Everyone would be better off without me," the Saboteur encouraged me each step of the way. I climbed to my departure spot, with a wonderful sense of accomplishment.

I climbed the wet, stone steps that led to the railway bridge, which crossed a busy main road in the centre of town. I bent down, picked up a cold stone and dropped it over the edge. "One....two....Plop!" I counted, knowing, thanks to my air force days, the height of the bridge would provide enough of a free fall to execute the task.

Stepping onto the edge of the bridge, I took one last deep breath and...

Just as I went to leap to my death, a double-decker bus came rumbling down the hill and under the bridge.

Suddenly, I snapped out of my somnambulistic state. "I could have been killed!" I thought. "What about the poor driver and passengers? What if I end up disabled and live? I'll be an even bigger burden!" The thoughts poured into my mind about living and being a liability to all of my family. "I can't even kill myself properly," I whispered, beginning to cry.

Walking home that night, I felt broken; body, mind, and soul. What followed were six long, long months of darkness; I had become a sobbing wretch of a man, where once I had been so full of hope and ambition. Part of me certainly did take a leap from the bridge and die that night, the corpse that I journeyed with during this time weighed very heavily upon my heart and soul.

Each day I stayed indoors, fearing visitors, crying spontaneously if the phone should ring. The Saboteur Within whispered that whole time, "No one can be trusted, not even your evil wife, and even she is plotting against you. She's not alone; everyone is in on the secret plan." Remember my master plan was to terminate my life, now here I was spinning inside my mind, tumbling within my universe, a dark prison of my own making. I needed to grab hold of something, anything! Just to allow me to re-connect, with my purpose. My Saboteur hadn't been given any new instructions and because I didn't know who I was, he continued the psychological barrage of dark, threatening imagery and disagreements.

Somewhere deep inside my higher consciousness, the watcher, was listening and set me a task, a simple task: to tidy the back garden. I can't even remember how I got started but bit-by-bit, I would dig and weed, day-by-day, little by little. Adding flowers here and there, thinking of nothing but the garden. Mr. Miyagi would have been proud of me as I blindly fumbled through the bleak and confusing haze that had once been my clear and joyous life.

Mr. Miyagi is a character in the movie "Karate Kid". Young Daniel is being bullied at school and so he wants to learn Karate so that he can defend himself. He eventually persuades Mr. Miyagi, a neighbour, to teach him. Every day he turns up expecting to learn the secrets of Karate and every day Mr. Miyagi simply gives him another task, sanding the floor, painting the fence, washing and waxing the cars. After about a month, Daniel flipped and accused Miyagi of not teaching him anything. Nothing could be further from the truth, Mr. Miyagi had taught Daniel lots of things! If you haven't seen the movie then I would encourage you to watch it, if you have seen it, then watch it again. There is much wisdom contained in that lighthearted film.

Meanwhile, back in my garden it was a long, lazy, sunny July evening. Joan, our neighbour looked over the fence and said, "You've done a lovely job of that garden, Matty." Upon hearing her voice, for the first time I looked up and saw the garden as a whole. Up to that point, I had only just been seeing whatever little patch I had been working at the time. As Joan spoke to me the blinkers fell from my eyes and I realised, that very slowly, little by little and bit-by-bit, I had transformed the whole garden.

It was right at that same moment that something inside my mind undoubtedly shifted, the confines of my own mental prison, fell away and Matt was born. Or, should I say, reborn!

For a long while after that July night I still felt broken, but I could now see the light at the end of the tunnel and felt confident that I was on the road to recovery from what was described to me as a nervous breakdown. In truth, I look back now with the realisation that Matty died that night on the bridge.

Eventually, like a phoenix from the ashes, I would return even stronger. I needed time to re-energise, regroup, and redefine myself. I guess you could say that it was during this period of recovery and regeneration that I lost the "why" questions and began a life long journey of discovering "how."

I had been to the very edge of my existence and returned a new me. Suddenly I had found a new purpose: people needed to know that there is an alternative way out of the dark **without drugs**. During the process, I elected to enlist my Saboteur and retrain him to support me on my quest.

∽

"Let Go of Your "Whys?" to Become Wise"

∽

Looking back now, the path that "Matty" was on might have been "okay," but it wasn't okay for "Matt." By letting go of the "Y" in my name, my life literally transformed; it was like shedding a skin to reveal the true me underneath!

Even now as I type, I am aware of the realisation that I had during that time. It was the "why?" questions that had been looping in my head that caused the dizzying, emotional, tail spin, and bad feelings in my stomach. I had been caught in the vicious circles that 'why?' questions engender, and that could never serve me.

It dawned on me that by asking "how?" questions, my mind would give me good information that would, in turn, give me a sense of direction and help me emerge from the darkness.

I find that a lot of conflict, whether at home or in the work place, begins when somebody begins to point the finger and start firing the "whys?" everywhere.

If you practice letting them go, your Saboteur will fall into line. If you don't, you will add strength to an already immense force, which can work against you, just as powerfully as it will support you when you are asking the right questions. How questions will help you identify the resources that you need which will enable you to break the spell of your viscous circle and move forward.

Example;

How can I get slimmer? Rather than, why am I fat?

How can I become smarter? Rather than, why am I stupid?

How............................?Why ....?

How can you begin to write your list? Rather than, why don't you make a list?

After that six months incubation whilst the real me began to develop my wings, I promised I would never take anything too seriously ever again.

My Saboteur was supporting me going down the wrong path, but now that I had a sense of purpose, he would accompany me on my road to recovery; keeping me aware that time and tide wait for no one.

❧

Exercise

"The only "Why" you will ever need"

In 2009, Simon Sinek released the book "Start With Why" – a synopsis of the theory he has begun using, to teach others how to become effective leaders and inspire change. This might sound like a total contradiction to what I have been saying but actually it parallels it.

Here is the 'Ted Talks' link: http://www.ted.com/talks/simon_sinek_how_great_leaders_inspire_action.html

Sinek suggests every single person on the planet knows "What they do", some know "how they do it" but only very few know "why they do it". The diagram below shows you what Sinek calls the Golden Circle, he says that most organisations and people work from the outside of the circle and move inwards, whereas great leaders, start with the "Why?" in the centre and work outwards. This is the difference that makes the difference. The warm, emotional, fuzzy stuff at the centre of the circle touches others and calls to us all.

Simon shows us how to engage, everyday with purpose by asking the question "Why do I do what I do?" or "Why do I get out of bed in the morning?" Please follow the link or buy his book, even better do both!

After discovering this wonderful guy I spent three days uncovering my own personal "Why statement" which is;

"Developing personal potential allows our world to evolve. By helping people create flexibility in their communications, they generate lasting change and I just happen to make it simple and fun!"

The Golden Circle

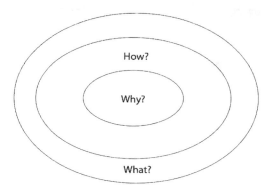

The statement above encapsulates why I do what I do and how I do it!

So your challenge is to write your own personal "Why statement". Call your friends round because it is a bit of a challenge. I found myself writing "what I did" and "how I did it" but with the help of my wife Sonya and son Karl, I nailed it. The funny thing is as I look at the statement now it really does sum up everything about me.

Now, I know why I get out of bed in the morning, I know the type of people I want to work with, and the sort of things that have to be present in order for me to be motivated!

I was working for an organisation recently that does a wonderful job of helping unemployed people back to work. During the few days I was with them, I looked at several CV's and noticed that they all spoke from the "what" position. Example; I am an honest person, a good timekeeper, I have experience in customer service, I have a clean driving license, etc, Not only did they all speak from "what" they all sounded the same.

"How on earth can an employer make a decision if everyone sounds the same?"

So here is an example of a "why statement":

"To earn through honest toil, should be the battle cry for all. Gaining financial independence allows me to set a great example for my children. You as an employer can give me the one chance that I need."

Can you feel the difference? Is it possible that the employer now has a greater sense of Who? What? How? When? And Why? This person is the one to talk to?

Once you've got your "Why statement" put it up on the wall and just let it hang around for a few days until you are absolutely comfortable with it.

You will then find yourself galvanized to your purpose; the watcher and your Saboteur will be in absolute alignment with you.

∽

Chapter 10

Chaos, Confusion & Infinite Possibilities
"Chaos is the score upon which reality is written"

Henry Miller

Change is different. That much is clear. And lasting change can be challenging; but living life thinking you are unloved, destined to be the fat sister etc. Is a life less lived. Take a look at your 'I Ams' and question your Saboteur. Dare to break out of the box and experience an amazing new you...

Chaos and Confusion is Scary

I believe you picked up this book because you wanted to change, because you suspected something is wrong with the way you're hardwired and because you're good and tired of the Saboteur Within always keeping you safe and sound in your small box...

Well, I can help, but you have to help yourself too. One way to do that is to face two simple facts about change:

1. **Change isn't hard, it's just <u>different</u>;**
2. **<u>Chaos</u> and <u>confusion</u> are part and parcel of change.**

Change is Different

Anyone who's ever tried to change – anything – knows that change can seem almost impossible. When, in fact, change is whatever you choose to believe. Think about it as "hard" and "difficult" or alternatively "exciting" and "powerful", either way, you will be right.

Therefore, thinking about it as "different" or "new" will get you through the uncomfortable bits more quickly and with less pain.

Quitting smoking, leaving a dysfunctional relationship, or changing your career may appear to be physically hard or a phenomenal challenge, but you have the power to decide how it will be for you.

Our lives are challenging enough without change, yet they'll only become more painful and uncomfortable if we don't change. For me to ask you to do something as fundamentally backward-seeming to you as "embrace chaos and confusion" sounds like the opposite of self-help, but in point of fact you wouldn't be here if you weren't ready for a little upheaval and reorganisation in your life!

I get it; we don't like chaos. It's unpleasant, it can be threatening and, frankly, we often work hard just to avoid it. But how much longer do you want to live believing that every guy is a waste of space? How much longer can you go on feeling unloved, unwanted, ugly or destined to be your family's version of the "black sheep"?

If you've been paying attention at all by now you'll know that problems don't just "go away" because they've reached an expiration date. If anything, if we don't address them and sweep them under the carpet, they only get worse as we go along.

It's not okay to give in to your Saboteur Within just because it feels the easiest route; your mind will always choose the path of least resistance. Where has that gotten you so far?

In order to break free of the limiting self-beliefs of your "I Am" statements about you and your life, you must be ready to change; you must be willing to enter into a place where, temporarily, chaos and confusion rule.

Chaos and Confusion Are Part and Parcel of Change

Picture a man who has an "I Am" statement that reads, "I Am 52-years-old and **already past my prime**." Imagine that; being 52 and already writing off the rest of your life, love, career, success or whatever else the next 40 years, or so, might bring him.

In his case, that "I Am" statement is not just a limiting self-belief; it's a social, spiritual, physical, financial, and professional death sentence. If you truly believe you are past your prime in your 50s, what do your 60s hold for you? To say nothing of your 70s, 80s, and even 90s?

What if Betty White believed she was past her prime? Or Kirk Douglas? Or Helen Mirren? Or any number of creative, healthy, successful, vibrant people for whom their 50s is just another step *up* the ladder, not down?

Now, take that same man, who has so much locked in potential, energy, youth, vitality and life to live and throw his "I Am" statement into chaos and confusion by rewriting it to read, "I Am 52 and **just entering my prime**!" Suddenly, he can't give up on life anymore! Instead, he has to go out there and live it, harder and faster, and with more creativity and challenge than ever before.

At first glance, it might appear that life is much simpler if you believe your best years are already behind you. Without new mountains to climb, challenges to overcome, obstacles to navigate our way around, or risks to take, we can just... rest easy. The truth is, once you open yourself up to chaos and confusion, you can live life more fully, more happily and with more satisfaction. Frankly, if you're unhappy with your life so far, you can't really start living until you step out of your comfort zone, face a little, temporary, chaos and confusion, and open up to the infinite possibilities of life outside the box

What the Mind Suppresses, the Body Expresses!

You have to shift your focus from the limited to the limitless. Stop seeing chaos and confusion as something to be avoided at all cost and see them as doorways to possibility! Yes, change can bring temporary complications that are often "inconvenient," but around the corner from them is the possibility for a life you've never even imagined, full of joy, creativity, love passion and all the things you've been hoping for yourself "someday."

Today can be your someday. But, you won't get it from your easy chair, from the sofa, from bed or from the comfort of your small "I Am" box.

Norman Cousins wrote the book *Anatomy of An Illness* (W. W. Norton & Company, 2001 [reissue]) almost 15 years after his terminal diagnosis in 1964. During his lifetime, Cousins was thrown into massive confusion when he contracted a life threatening disease known as "ankylosing spondylitis," a degenerative disease that causes the breakdown of collagen, the fibrous tissue that binds together the body's cells.

Cousins was nearly totally paralyzed and given only a few months to live, when he discharged himself from the hospital, moved into a hotel room and prescribed himself massive amounts of vitamin C and overwhelming amounts of humour.

Norman knew that he had to do something radical if he was to survive. And if the medical profession were right and certain of his prognosis, what did he have to lose? He realised that he must take responsibility for his own health and well-being and he did so in a style that would earn him great praise from many professionals around the world, making him the man who laughed himself back to health. They even made a movie about him, check it out; it's still available on DVD and well worth watching.

WARNING: *You Are Entering Consciously Uncharted Territory!*

Letting go of all that is familiar can be scary and terrifying, but just imagine all that's out there waiting for you. Once upon a time everyone thought the world was flat; that if you sailed out past a certain distance in the sea you would literally fall off the face of the earth and that was that!

Imagine being one of the first explorers to test that theory – talk about chaos, confusion, and fear!!! And now, imagine being the first to experience the infinite possibility of a world that is round and full of amazing, breathtaking new lands.

What you need is proof; proof that the world isn't flat, that your box is actually a prison and change can be liberating! Let's say your "I Am" statement is that you are a "happily married" woman. Well, how come you are not enjoying life? Why are you feeling cold toward your spouse, or you get the sense that he's a little chilly towards you?

Could it be your marriage is not so happy after all? Could you be missing some hard evidence that your Saboteur has been deleting? – Late nights, having to work the weekend, lipstick on a collar or two – Are you beginning to suspect that your 'I am happily married' is actually an out of date 'I am' statement?

When a seemingly happily married woman discovers her husband is cheating on her; wham, suddenly there is a massive "I Am" shift and lots of chaos comes flooding in. Now, "I am an unhappily married woman" is your new norm.

But… but… but your system, your Saboteur, your unconscious may well seek to delete, generalise and distort in an attempt to support your old 'I Am' and have you stay in an unhealthy relationship just to keep you in your chosen box. Alternatively, whilst caught in the tidal wave of this new information, she could choose to develop a new 'I Am' and open up all kinds of new opportunities, you just have to be brave enough to live in chaos for a while, allowing yourself to transform and grow into your new 'I Am'

∽

Parting Words About Chaos, Confusion and Infinite Possibilities

"When we are no longer able to change a situation –
We are challenged to change ourselves"
Victor E. Frankl

Literally, the possibilities are endless. All because you faced chaos and confusion, even if it's involuntarily, to come out the other side and explore life's ultimate, endless and truly infinite possibilities!

When people go through that transformation, and into infinite possibilities, their energy gets better, their body feels better; they now have the option to pick a brand new "I Am."

∽

Chapter 11

Enlisting your Saboteur
We dance round in a ring and suppose,
But the secret sits in the middle and knows
Robert Frost

There are certain times when you can sit back in the stillness of your mind and just wonder where in the world you are? When I say you I'm not talking about the flesh and bone vehicle that you are currently travelling in, no, I mean the real you! Listen, right now and you can hear yourself reading these words but where are you as you listen?

Are you the listener or are you the speaker?

Take your time to consider this and as you do, I would like to offer you yet another position, that of the watcher. Because you are watching as you listen to yourself speaking, are you not?

What if your watcher deploys your Saboteur, greater you that has all of the answers, intrinsically connected to you and the rest of the universe simultaneously?

I wanted to find a way of engaging with the watcher, understanding what purpose he holds for me, aligning my consciousness with that purpose, and therefore, utilising the Saboteur to support me.

∽

So without any further ado, here is the exercise-

The Saboteur Within Exercise

You will need a coach or a friend, five pieces of paper and a little bit of room to walk around.
Steps:
Take five pieces of paper, which will represent the following:

a) This is where you are now
b) This is your goal or desired outcome
c) This is your Saboteur
d) These are your resources
e) These are even more resources

Place a) on the floor and get a sense of where you are right now.
Next walk forward and place your goal out in front of you, then return to a).

Next, Place c) your Saboteur anywhere you wish between a) and b).

Next, Notice do you self sabotage early, half way or just before you could attain your goal?

1. Move your Saboteur to the left, so that you can see your goal clearly.
2. Place your resources d) and e) where you want them.
3. Walk to your goal and stepping on d) and e) as you go and taking the time to fully access your resources.

Next, Step to the side and see yourself achieving your goal with your resources.

1. Go back to the start point and bring your Saboteur back into line with a), b), d) and e).
2. Take a step into the first resources; fully experience what those resources allow you to do.
3. Take a step into your Saboteur. What do you experience?
4. Ask the Saboteur, what is his/her positive intention behind being there?
5. Ask your Saboteur if he/she is willing to work with you to get to the goal.
6. Bring all the resources from the Saboteur inside of you.
7. Take a step onto e) your second resources and add them to your journey.
8. Take a step into your goal and how does it feel. What do you experience?

Step to the side and fully experience your journey to your goal.

View from the watchers position and connect to the universe, allow yourself permission to remain connected as you appoint your Saboteur, to support you, whilst you take full responsibility for yourself.

Hold that position and feel the love flooding through you, you are awesome!

I have used this exercise in different countries, with many different cultures and guess what? Everyone knows, instinctively, at which point he or she will sabotage himself or herself!

If you sit here hypothesising you won't get it, but as soon as you lay the pieces down in front of you, the watcher is allowed to engage with you.

Some people put the Saboteur down close to them, which means that they never really get started and subsequently never set goals, because they are unachievable.

Some people put the Saboteur down at about half way, so they've gotten half way to succeeding and the Saboteur de-rails them. With "It's just not for me" "who was I kidding!"

My heart goes out to the final group who put the Saboteur down just before they reach their goal. Imagine that, if you will, you have struggled night and day for months on end, overcoming huge obstacles, slaying dragons and demons en route, only to quit when the end is insight!

∽

For all of you I would like to offer this poem, which can keep a fire burning in you. The author of this poem was so amazing that he or she didn't even sign it, that is what I call leaving an impression.

"When things go wrong, as they sometimes will,
When the road you're trudging seems all uphill,
When the funds are low and the debts are high,
And you want to smile, but you have to sigh,
When care is pressing you down a bit,
Rest, if you must, but don't you quit.
Life is queer with its twists and turns,
As every one of us sometimes learns,
And many a failure turns about,
When he might have won had he stuck it out;
Don't give up though the pace seems slow–
You may succeed with another blow.
Often the goal is nearer than,
it seems to a faint and faltering man,
Often the struggler has given up,

When he might have captured the victor's cup,
And he learned too late when the night slipped down,
How close he was to the golden crown.
Success is failure turned inside out–
The silver tint of the clouds of doubt,
And you never can tell how close you are,
It may be near when it seems so far,
So stick to the fight when you're hardest hit–
It's when things seem worst that you must not quit."

- Author unknown

Epilogue

"Without change, something sleeps inside us, and seldom awakens. The sleeper must awaken"

Frank Herbert

Finally, we've come to the end of our journey! But don't fret; this is the best chapter of all. Why? Because this is where you learn to keep your friends close, and **your enemy closer**!

This book has not been about killing off your Saboteur, or beating him/her into submission; use him for your own good! Remember, at the end of the day, the Saboteur Within is there to protect you. It doesn't think, it just does; it's like a mercenary, hired to do a job no matter what that job is.

Never misinterpret me to think that "I Am" statements are necessarily "bad" things; only when they're self-limiting do such statements hold us back. In the last chapter, "I am an unhappily married woman" led to chaos and confusion, which ultimately led to a NEW "I Am" statement – "I Am a happily single woman" – that led to happiness, challenge and infinite possibilities.

So the goal becomes not to kill off the Saboteur but to use that energy, power and capacity of the unconscious mind to rewrite your "I Am" statement and use the Saboteur to protect and defend it in a positive, uplifting way.

Consider how the following "I Am" statements can be turned around and used for good:

- **By switching "I Am... <u>a smoker</u>" with "I Am... <u>a non-smoker</u>," you can finally focus on using the Saboteur Within to protect your non-smoking habits.**
- **By switching "I Am... <u>the dumb one in the family</u>" with "I Am... <u>a student in college</u>," you can finally focus on using the Saboteur Within to ensure you study hard and pass your exams.**
- **By switching "I Am... <u>an unhappily married woman</u>" with "I Am... <u>a happily single lady</u>," you can finally focus on using the Saboteur Within to support you in your new life on the dating scene.**

By switching "I Am... <u>unlovable</u>" with "I Am... <u>lovable</u>," you can finally focus on using the Saboteur Within to firmly protect your lovable new self. Your Saboteur will now stop you embarking on another disastrous relationship and will now only let you choose a lovable, loving and caring partner.

- **By switching your "I Am... <u>an overeater</u>" with "I Am... <u>a healthy eater</u>," you can finally focus on using the Saboteur Within to protect your healthy eating habits and ensure you maintain a fabulous, trim figure.**

See how that works? For most of this book we've addressed the unconscious mind; the Saboteur Within and how it can create havoc and heartbreak if allowed to run amok, enforcing out of date and out of place rules and restrictions.

Think about it; this is powerful, powerful stuff. Imagine the enemy, the most powerful weapon in the world! It was decimating your forces, wiping out all your troops and there was no way to combat it unless… you send in a super-duper secret spy team to steal it and bring it back to your side. Now you can use the enemy's greatest weapon against itself and win.

In this case, your enemy is the old self-limiting "I Am" statement you've been living with for years; I am unlovable, I am stupid, I am meant to be fat, I am a smoker and so on and so on.

And the ultimate weapon, of course, is the Saboteur Within; who is so strong and powerful that the only way to defeat it is to acknowledge it, capture it and reprogram it to protect your new "I Am" statement!

By using the exercise in this book and working with a friend/coach you can redefine who you are, develop a whole new set of "I Am" statements and then put your Saboteur in charge of enforcing them.

I am aware it's not always easy. That's why most smokers quit for a little while, then go back. It's why most diets fail and in fact, many people gain more than they lost in the first place. It's why women who feel unloved are so resistant to trusting a new man that they typically revert to their old habits of driving him away before they can get hurt again. It's why millions of people stay in dead-end jobs rather than taking that chance of embracing the entrepreneur within. But it is doable!

One factor that plays heavily in change is giving ourselves the time to change. Remember in the last chapter when I introduced **The Three Keys to Transformation:**

1. You have to **want to change**
2. You have to **know how to change**
3. You have to have **the time to change**

I know that you want to change; and now you know how to change. The key is to focus on the third aspect of transformation: give yourself the time to change! Remember, there is no expiration date on success, there is no deadline for self-actualisation and, ultimately, the only person you need to please is yourself.

I would like to add an extra piece right about now and that is **<u>Give yourself permission to change.</u>**

Many clients that I have been fortunate enough to work with have found that "permission" can truly set them free to change. Case in point: Leslie and Carol were both diagnosed with the same type of cancer and both had the same prognosis. Many years later they were both still alive and kicking and yet Leslie had needed much more chemo and additional treatments whilst Carol had made a rapid and uncomplicated recovery. Although the two ladies had inspired each other along the way, Leslie felt bad that she wasn't recovering as quickly as her comrade.

We worked around the rules laid out in this book and very quickly found that Leslie still held a grudge against someone in her early childhood and hadn't forgiven him for what he had done.

I explained that I wasn't able to change her past, but would work with her to change her perception of it. Remember, each thought has a chemical reaction and here was Leslie, 50 years later, still being fed those same poisonous thoughts, deep inside her unconscious mind, courtesy of her Saboteur. All of those toxic thoughts about Leslie not being "whole" were being nurtured and they, in turn, would manifest in to the very thing that she feared most.

It's maddening when you think about it, isn't it? There you are wandering around thinking about the terrible thing that you never want to happen to you and BHAM! You open your eyes one day and hey presto! It's yours!!!

Stop thinking about what you don't want, because you will only enlist your Saboteur to go out and get it for you!

Think about what you do want and let that take up your energy.

Focus on rewriting your "I Am" statements and enlist the Saboteur Within to support you. The keys to success are all inside you; you just have to give yourself permission to set them free!

Hopefully, this book has given you the tools you need to unleash and harness the power of your Saboteur Within!

Final Words

Congratulations if you have gotten this far and have taken the time to get to know yourself, more. If you have whizzed through the book only searching for gold, on the surface, I hope you got what you wanted. The gems, however, are buried a little deeper and that is why I suggested that you have a friend or a coach support you.

Everyone that I've spoken to during the research of my book have commented upon the title; each of us on some level recognise the Saboteur Within. I put off finishing this book for years, whilst my Dad was alive, because I told him that he couldn't go until he had read my book! I used not finishing as a means of keeping him alive that was unfair, "Dad, I know you missed my mam terribly and that you are both happier now."

Shelle Rose Charvet and I were in a coaching session, when Shelle asked me "What did finishing this book mean to me?" I felt a weight inside my chest as I saw a gravestone inside my mind. Somehow I had equated completion with my death! And then I was wondering what was preventing me from getting on with writing? What seemed like self-sabotage was really self-preservation! My mind had made an association between "completion" and the absolute completion of my life, which I am happy to say, will continue for many years to come. You will be able to find out more, when I release my next book, "Is That Why You Do This?" Which is about the rules that were alive and kicking when you were growing up inside your family home.

Thank you to my family, friends and to you, whom if we never meet face to face, we have met soul to soul.

Live a simple life and have fun!

∽

"You have the Answer.
Just get quiet enough to hear it"
Pat Obuchowski

∽

To learn more you can contact me here
www.thesaboteurwithin.com

Printed in Great Britain
by Amazon.co.uk, Ltd.,
Marston Gate.